Executive's Guide to Internet Law

Sheila A. Millar

asae | american society of
association executives

Washington, DC

Information in this book is accurate as of the time of publication and consistent with standards of good practice in the general management community. As research and practice advance, however, standards may change. For this reason, it is recommended that readers evaluate the applicability of any recommendation in light of particular situations and changing standards.

This book is intended to provide information of general interest to associations related to their Internet activities. It is not intended as legal advice for particularized facts. The Internet is a fast-evolving medium, and recommendations on how to handle specific questions may change quickly as well. You should consult a lawyer if you have legal questions requiring attention.

American Society of Association Executives
1575 I Street, NW
Washington, DC 20005-1103
Phone: (202) 626-2723
Fax: (202) 408-9634
E-mail: books@asaenet.org
ASAE's core purpose is to advance the value of voluntary associations to society and to support the professionalism of the individuals who lead them.

Susan Robertson, Vice President, Marketing and Communications
Anna Nunan, Director of Book Publishing
Louise Quinn, Acquisitions Coordinator
Jennifer Moon, Production Manager
Anthony Conley, Operations Coordinator

Cover design by Joyce C. Weston and interior design by Black Dot Group.

This book is available at a special discount when ordered in bulk quantities. For information, contact the ASAE Member Service Center at (202) 371-0940.

A complete catalog of titles is available on the ASAE Web site at www.asaenet.org/bookstore

Table of Contents

About the Author

Sheila A. Millar is a partner in the law firm of Keller and Heckman LLP, Washington, D.C. She counsels corporate and association clients on e-commerce, product liability, antitrust, contract, insurance, and regulatory compliance issues. She works with corporate and association clients to assist them in generating revenues and promoting their brands online through both business-to-business and business-to-consumer activities. Millar helps clients develop privacy policies, data security and access procedures, as well as training programs to assure compliance, and advocates on their behalf on a range of e-commerce issues before key policy bodies. She counsels clients on intellectual property and advertising issues and assists them in structuring intellectual property protection programs to protect their trademarks and copyrights. Millar also works with clients to navigate the array of federal and state requirements related to contests and sweepstakes.

Millar negotiates Web hosting, Web development and e-commerce agreements, and helps clients adapt their business models to the fast-changing world of e-commerce. She also develops Web disclaimers and user agreements to meet applicable legal requirements related to advertising and product liability concerns and to address jurisdiction and venue issues related to e-commerce.

In addition, Millar counsels clients on risk management and product safety matters for both industrial and consumer products, as well as on compliance with Consumer Product Safety Commission requirements. She has special expertise in all issues related to the sale and marketing of children's products. Millar's environmental regulatory expertise includes ozone depletion, global warming, clean air matters, pesticides, and solid waste. She has been involved in the establishment of joint research ventures under the antitrust laws to address environmental issues.

Millar holds a B.A. from Bryn Mawr College, and a J.D. from American University.

Acknowledgments

The author gratefully acknowledges the contributions of her partner, Peter de la Cruz, to the chapter on antitrust, and of G. Brent Mickum to the chapter on online sweepstakes. Vanessa H. Broussard and R. Holland Campbell also assisted. Special thanks to Joan E. Cohen for her invaluable research and editorial assistance and to our support staff.

I. INTRODUCTION

A. Benefits of the Internet

E-commerce has exploded. U.S. retail purchases over the Internet totaled $5.52 billion during the second quarter of 2000, according to recent Commerce Department figures. Ad spending hit $5 billion and is predicted to reach $16 billion by 2005.[1] Business-to-business (B2B) sales were over $2 billion in 1999 and should reach $5 trillion by 2004.[2] E-commerce offerings exist or are being developed in almost every sector of the economy, although at a much slower pace in recent months as the once sizzling technology economy has cooled down.

Trade associations and other nonprofits have not been immune to this outbreak of "dot-com fever," a sometimes crippling or even fatal ailment for organizations that make incorrect or misguided business or legal decisions. With the dot-com bubble bursting economically, it is especially important for associations to understand the business and legal issues of the Internet. Unless they do, they will be unable to maximize the advantages of the World Wide Web to enhance existing services and to create new services for their members.

The recent spate of dot-com failures is due to a variety of complex factors. Skyrocketing stock prices not justified by revenues, much less profits, is one key reason. Another is the failure by many Internet companies to develop a vision of customer service or "value-added" to customers. E-businesses that are succeeding,

---

[1] Jupiter Online Advertising Forum 2000, Aug. 25, 2000.
[2] *Wall Street Journal*, July 12, 1999, p. R6.

whether they are pure online firms or hybrid "clicks and mortars" businesses, use the Internet to create value and serve their customers. These businesses are looking strategically at how to integrate the Internet into their product and service offerings. It is a lesson that should not be forgotten by associations considering new or expanded Internet ventures.

The stock in trade for most nonprofits is *information*. Associations early on recognized the potential of the Internet to streamline information and reduce mailing and printing expenses. This opportunity for cost savings is vital for trade associations at a time when so many industry sectors are going through consolidation, often with an adverse result on dues, trade show, conference and other sources of association income. It is equally vital for other nonprofits that wish to devote the maximum resources possible to their charitable and educational initiatives. Yet the vast explosion of information available on the Internet risks making associations obsolete. Your members can find out events and developments of interest to them from an array of external sources. Your viability depends on your ability to target your members—your customers—and to provide them with the right information, in the right format, and at the right intervals, that is best suited to the member needs.

The Internet and other electronic communications vehicles help you deliver the type of targeted information your members want and need, cutting through the clutter of the mass of information on the Internet. E-mail updates and alerts allow associations to get information on government relations issues, technical news, association events (like conferences, trade shows, and meetings), standards, statistics, and important industry or media trends to members quickly and cheaply. Web-based statistical reporting programs make faster reporting possible by members. Faster reporting of data into the organization expedites the process of compiling the antitrust-appropriate reports back to participants and can be structured to minimize confidentiality concerns. Web-enabled meetings may allow participants to remotely work on important documents, like position papers or standards, and online purchase and registration opportunities may result in cost savings for the association. And association Web sites offer a venue to advance public relations, government relations, and membership objectives outside their immediate membership ranks.

The Internet allows associations to inform the public, government agencies, and others about their industry, to provide nonmembers a glimpse of the benefits they are missing by not belonging to the organization, and to provide special members-only areas where additional details and inside information on cutting edge topics is available. Some nonprofit organizations (often arts and environmental organizations) are also using the Internet to allow both members and members of the public to make online purchases of merchandise. Many times merchandise contains the association logo, and posted prices may show special discounts for members.

In addition, e-businesses as well as traditional businesses are seeking to partner with associations in a variety of e-commerce opportunities. The reasons are fairly simple. Associations often have well-recognized brand names and offer the perfect outlet for the type of targeted and relationship marketing that is the lifeblood of the interactive world. Web marketers, especially those whose business models rely on advertising, are looking for "hits" or visitors, with a primary goal being the generation of traffic at the site—and the diversion of visitors to their own sites. The Web offers associations an ability to promote special membership discounts on selected products or services. The *quid pro quo* has typically involved promises about the generation of nondues revenues for the association. Many of these arrangements have failed to achieve the level of income promised to associations. The collapse of the dot-com industry in the beginning of 2001 will likely have an impact on these ventures. Because few associations have realized the income promised, the anticipated slowdown in growth of these ventures will provide time for associations to truly consider their objectives in the e-market world. The astute association with defined goals, defined member needs, and clearly thought out objectives should still be able to negotiate arrangements that offer direct and indirect value—financial and otherwise—to the association and its members. These are the association business partners likely to be most attractive to outside ventures.

B. Overview of Legal Issues

The Internet brings with it some thorny and unresolved legal and business questions on issues like jurisdiction and choice of law, privacy and security, as well as new challenges involving old topics like intellectual property (IP) protection, antitrust compliance, and minimization of liability. Valuing the association's intellectual capital and maintaining the association's independent identity and integrity in attempting to negotiate a variety of dot-com deals can also be a tricky business. Some associations make the fatal mistake of either over- or underestimating what they bring to the table. Others jump into ill-advised arrangements seduced by some up-front cash into giving long-term exclusive endorsements to Internet ventures that are likely to fail. The relative lack of definitive precedents for B2B paradigms makes it difficult to evaluate the viability of possible business partners or the validity of their projections about revenues. Often associations do not recognize that old paradigms of doing business (and old contractual approaches) are simply inadequate in this brave new world.

This primer, while not intended to provide specific legal advice on particularized facts, provides a general overview of the most important questions which associations must deal with when offering a Web site or when engaged in e-commerce. Legal challenges for associations currently involve several major topics.

First, IP issues and strategies are vital to associations. Too many associations neglect to adopt appropriate IP protection strategies offline. Neglect could be fatal online. Your content and your name are your most important assets and in the click and paste world of the Web can be readily stolen. IP is one of the most central elements of success on the Web, and failing to protect your IP may marginalize your organization.

Second, e-business strategies depend on an array of new and different agreements, like Web development agreements, maintenance and host agreements, Web distribution agreements, and linking and other e-commerce agreements. Endorsement/linking agreements are increasing in importance as dot-coms and other businesses, recognizing the need to turn Web visitors into e-commerce purchasers, look to ways to use associations to target customers for themselves. Exclusivity and noncompete issues, data access rights (and related privacy considerations), compensation models, IP protections, and liability limiting provisions are typical issues in these agreements.

Third, as with all association offline activities, antitrust considerations must be factored into the structure of association Internet activities. This is especially important for associations considering various types of B2B e-commerce opportunities where members buy and sell products and services to each other, or to customer or supplier groups. The ownership and structure of the arrangement, exclusivity aspects, minimum or maximum purchase requirements, and management/equity aspects are only some of the issues that might be raised. Many arrangements, of course, can be structured, using contracts, bylaws, and other operational documents, to readily address antitrust concerns. This may simply mean putting into operation existing antitrust compliance programs already in effect for the association. In some instances, however, it may be prudent or even necessary to seek a business review letter from antitrust authorities before proceeding with certain e-ventures.

Fourth, privacy has emerged as a key legal and media issue, generating almost daily headlines about some lapse, either real or perceived, in how personal information is handled. Yet, while about 90% of major U.S. commercial Web sites have now posted privacy statements, few associations do. Relatedly, security of personal data and information, including credit card data, and confidential information submitted by members, is essential to assure confidence in your Web-based activities. Security issues are also a concern in structuring B2B activities to be sure that members making purchases on the Web site are appropriately authorized to do so, and transaction data remains confidential. Indeed, with polls showing that privacy is a major public concern, and identity theft on the rise, addressing the security of data—particularly financial or credit card data—is of central importance. Investing in appropriate security is part and parcel of maintaining your brand value as an association.

Fifth, liability minimization continues to be a major objective of associations at a time when there is a perception of a slight increase in liability exposure for association standards and other activities. New antitrust challenges are posed not only by B2B ventures, but also by association Web sites that offer chat features. Chat rooms, message boards, and bulletin boards can be opportunities for members to improperly exchange information in violation of antitrust laws. Libel, defamation, and product disparagement issues may also arise in the Web environment. At the same time, one of the most enduring values of the Internet is the sense of community that develops with Web users, who are attracted to opportunities to interact via specific content areas that attract other visitors with similar interests and values.

The seamless nature of the Internet and ability to link from site to site is another unique aspect of the Internet that raises new legal issues. Care must be taken to establish that linking arrangements to members and others are not an endorsement of the linked site, for example. And, review by counsel of claims about products or services remains an important liability-limiting tool online, just as it does offline. The fast-paced nature of the Internet with its pressure to constantly post new content may tempt some to short-circuit approval mechanisms, potentially leading to exaggerated statements which could expand the organization's liability.

Finally, and most important, no clear answer yet exists to the question of what law or laws apply to activities on the Internet. This has implications for every legal issue associated with association Web activities.

In a recent *Harvard Business Review* article, the author notes that too many companies, "forgetting what they stand for or what makes them unique . . . have rushed to implement hot Internet applications and copy the offerings of dot-coms."[3] The associations that remember their unique mission and values are the ones that will likely survive and thrive in the Internet age.

---

[3]"Strategy and the Internet," Michael E. Porter, *Harvard Business Review*, March 2001

II. WEB IP ISSUES

Doing business on the Internet typically requires close attention to intellectual property issues. Much confusion exists about the differences between trademarks, copyrights, and patents. For example, we often hear people talk about "copyrighting" a logo (typically subject to trademark protection, not copyright protection). Your "brand" name will attract visitors to your site, making the selection of your domain name and your trademark protection strategies critical. And, at the heart of your Web site is your content. *Making sure you own or have appropriate rights to that content is vital.* This implicates copyright — both your own copyrights and those of third parties. Moreover, Web sites are built on a complex array of software and hardware, almost always developed by third parties. Hardware, software, and processes implicate patent rights. The bottom line: On the Web, you must negotiate and understand your IP rights (and the rights of others) to protect your organization—and your members. Never simply assume that your ad agencies, logo design firms, and interactive firms are taking all the necessary steps to "clear" the IP. And remember: Rights to contributions by consultants, contractors, and members must be contractually established in some circumstances to fully protect the organization from a copyright standpoint.

One useful tool to consider is a baseline Intellectual Property Audit that assesses the status of all IP owned, licensed, or in the process of development by the association. An audit will help associations identify the IP they own or use, can function as a measure of the value of their IP, and, equally important, can expose holes in an association's management of its valuable intellectual capital. Of course, an understanding of IP is neces-

6

sary to initiate a baseline audit, and periodic review and updates are needed to maintain its ongoing value. The following quick summary of IP issues is designed to simply be an overview of the issues.

A. Domain Names

Doing business on the Web typically starts with selection of a domain name. This is your "address" which will allow visitors around the world to find you on the World Wide Web. While the use of ".org" is conventionally associated with non-profit organizations, many associations have had to adopt ".com" or even ".net" domain names because similar terms were already taken.

Domain names are not necessarily trademarks, although they may function as trademarks if they actually identify your goods or services, and otherwise qualify as a trademark by indicating the source or origin of products or services. The first rule of domain name selection, then, is that you may not use another person's trademark as a domain name. This may not only constitute trademark infringement, but may also violate so-called anti-cybersquatting rules developed to prohibit abuses in domain name reservation.

The flip side of this rule is that the World Wide Web creates a push for adoption of simple, descriptive, or generic terms for ease of searching. Names like "grocery.com" will be incapable of obtaining trademark protection because they are simply generic names, but often have appeal as they are simple and easily found on search engines. Association names are often descriptive anyway, which actually may create a problem in trademark registration absent the inclusion of a logo or design. The bottom line is that associations need to consider domain name and trademark protection strategies carefully, as registration of a mark will provide benefits in dealing with cybersquatters.

The widespread problem of cybersquatting resulted in extraordinary numbers of complaints by trademark owners who were being held-up for ransom by "netrepreneurs" who were reserving trademarks as domain names and then attempting to sell them back to the rightful trademark owner, often for extraordinary sums of money. Congress enacted the Anti-Cybersquatting Consumer Protection Act[4] to address this concern, and the case law to date has in the vast majority of instances found in favor of the rightful trademark owner and against the so-called cybersquatter. Similarly, the Internet Corporation for Assigned Names and Numbers (ICANN), which is taking over the domain name assignment process, adopted a new uniform domain name dispute resolution policy, effective early in 2000. That process, which is a global one, offers an alternative dispute resolution mechanism for trademark owners to resolve complaints about trademark infringement associated with domain name registration. To prevail, a trademark

---

[4]Pub. L. No 106–113, 113 Stat. 1536, signed into Law Nov. 29, 1999; codified at 15 U.S.C. § 1114 *et seq.*

owner must prove that: 1) the contested domain name is identical or confusingly similar to a trade or service mark which he/she owns; 2) the domain name holder has no rights or legitimate interest in the domain name; and 3) a domain name was registered and is being used in bad faith. As is the case with the Anti-Cyber-squatting Act, most rulings to date favor the trademark owner.

B. Trademark Use and Registration

While a comprehensive review of trademark use and registration techniques is beyond the scope of this book, there are a few points to remember. The United States has adopted a system where trademark protection may be based on common law use as well as registration with the U.S. Patent and Trademark Office. The U.S. system of "first to use" is quite different from the "first to file" trademark protection rules in place throughout much of the world. Federal registration confers some significant benefits on the trademark owner, and should always be considered for important association marks. These benefits include:

> the presumption that you are the owner and that the mark is valid throughout the United States

> the ability to use the registration symbol, ®. It is prohibited by law for those who do not have a federally registered mark to use this symbol.

> the right to sue in federal court

> the ability to obtain "incontestability" after five years, limiting the grounds on which your mark can be canceled

> the ability to recover attorney's fees and up to treble damages for intentional infringement

> the ability to ask U.S. Customs Service officials to halt the import of infringing or counterfeit goods

> priority treatment in registering the mark abroad[5]

Trademarks and service marks must be registered in relevant International Classes. Most association trademarks are registered in Class 42 (for association services)[6], Class 41 (educational services), or in the collective membership and certification mark categories. Other International Classes may be relevant depending on the organization's activities, particularly Class 16 (publications).

Internet activities may create the need to not only consider but also to actively pursue foreign trademark registration options as associations, like many other businesses, go global. You should use the appropriate trademark indicia (™ for unregistered trademarks, SM for unregistered service marks, or ® for registered

---

[5]Lanham Act-15 USCA §§ 1051–1127.
[6]Remember to include in your description of services language that covers use of your mark on the World Wide Web.

marks) for all of your marks on your Web site,[7] and it is advisable to at least consider U.S. trademark registration for your key trade and service marks. Increasingly, the Internet also raises issues often unfamiliar to most associations: the desirability of foreign trademark and domain name registration in an increasingly global environment. Registration may be more expensive outside the United States and your objectives, costs, and benefits must be weighed carefully.

Associations must also remember the limits of trademark protection. Associations must typically "disclaim" most of the wording of their marks because the wording is considered to be "descriptive" apart from the mark as a whole. Neither an association nor a member of an industry or group may claim exclusive rights to common descriptive terms, but those "disclaimed" words are nevertheless protected as part of your mark as a whole.

Some associations encourage members to use a membership mark. Others, concerned about potential liability, prohibit members from placing the organization's logo on member products or advertising. These types of restrictions can be outlined in special logo guidelines, in membership applications, or even in trademark license agreements. (Formal agreements can be especially useful in controlling use of your certification marks.) These guidelines or agreements should include some reference to whether (and if so, how) the association's logo may appear on members' Internet sites. Licensing arrangements may also offer opportunities to generate nondues revenues through the sale of merchandise containing your marks.

As a practical matter, however, despite the limited ability to prevent other organizations from using key descriptive terms that may be part of your association's name by virtue of trademark registration, registration can certainly provide benefits in preventing other entities from misusing your mark, particularly in the event of cybersquatting. And registration is essential for organizations seeking to generate revenues from selling merchandise containing their logo or offering certification programs. The certification context is particularly important, as "counterfeiting" your certification mark could result in defective products and enhanced liability. This also means that you must initiate a trademark enforcement program to protect your rights as part of your liability minimization strategy.

C. Linking and Framing

Two technological applications in particular have become problematic for trademark owners: linking and framing. Associations, like any other organization on the Web, need to be aware of the legal issues.

What put the "Web" in World Wide Web are virtual transportation systems called "links," "hyperlinks" or "hotlinks." Links consist of highlighted words,

---

[7]Failure to do so risks an inability to recover attorney's fees, a potentially serious financial problem even with for-profit enterprises.

underlined text, or icons. Links allow seamless movement over the World Wide Web by simple clicks of the mouse. The Internet user could literally spend hours traveling through hyperlinks that began with a single link. Associations are often appealing business "partners" to other businesses because association sites serve as magnets for their members. That makes your Web site attractive to those who want to try to reach your membership by having your organization post a link that allows association members and other visitors to your site to travel directly to the linked site. Links can offer value and convenience to Web site visitors, but links should be authorized and associations should use care to avoid any statement or implication that they endorse the content of the linked site—even member or chapter sites. Linking policies with chapters or regional offices may be dependent on the relationship between the "parent" and the chapter organizations.

Compensation issues in linking agreements will likely differ depending on the organizational framework, member needs, and type of entity seeking a link. It is generally useful to structure compensation for linking in the form of a royalty or sponsorship fee. Nevertheless, compensation received for linking may raise an unrelated business income tax (UBIT) issue.

Framing is a variant of linking that often raises significant trademark issues. A typical Internet screen may be comprised of several subframes appearing within the larger frame of the screen. The technique of framing is a method by which content from one site is linked into another site and presented within a border. For example, a page in a Web-based business magazine may frame running stock quotes from NASDAQ®. What is most interesting and most problematic about framing is that the owner of Web site A may retrieve information from Web site B, and put it into a frame on Web site A without permission from B. Depending upon the manner in which this is done, the Internet user on Web site A may or may not know that some of the information presented originates (or, in Web parlance, is "retrieved") from Web site B, and may assume that B approves of, endorses, or is involved in developing the content at site A.

Trademark and copyright infringement (or contributory infringement) may occur when source indicators are omitted from the retrieved site, or where the retrieving site does not have permission to use the content (including advertising, if applicable)[8]. Where trademarks and/or advertisements are omitted from a retrieved site, the retrieved information may appear to come from the site onto which the user is logged, when in reality it comes from a completely different site. For many e-businesses, one of the more serious issues associated with this practice is that it can also have a significant negative impact on the advertising revenue of the retrieved party's site, if that site contains advertising.

---

[8]*See Futuredontics, Inc. v. Applied Anagramics, Inc.,* 45 USPQ2d (BNA) 2005, 1998 U.S. Dist. LEXIS 2265 (C.D. Cal. Feb. 3, 1998).

Some associations, looking for avenues to generate nondues income, accept advertising on their Web sites. Advertising revenues are often measured by the number of "hits" a particular Web site receives. Web sites that receive more hits can demand a higher price for the placement of advertisements on their sites. Linking and framing each raise distinct problems in this context. For instance, if an individual arrives directly at an internal page of a Web site through a link, a hit may not be recorded. Thus, the Web page operator may not accurately record the number of visitors accessing the Web site, the result of which may be a significant loss in advertising revenue. Framing presents an almost reciprocal problem. The advertiser who has paid a premium to appear on a site may have its advertising stripped out by a Web page operator who imports certain page content but not the surrounding advertising. Claims for copyright and trademark infringement have followed instances of framing.[9] That is one reason why permission for linking and framing is needed.

While linking and framing are not *per se* violative of the law, some uses of links or frames may constitute trademark or copyright infringement, trademark dilution, or unfair competition. As the law emerges, trademark owners and Web site designers should work closely with counsel when structuring links or frames to outside sites to avoid a possible infringing or diluting use of another's IP. Associations should obtain permission for linking and framing activities and establish policies on links by member companies to your site. Similarly, an association that spots an objectionable use of a link or frame involving the association's own trademarks or proprietary information should contact counsel immediately to explore the possible legal remedies available. Additionally, associations should consider requiring linking license agreements and possibly charge a fee for the use of the association logo by members. Linking license provisions are also a good idea when associations enter into business arrangements with for-profit entities for Web distribution of third-party products or services, or other B2B arrangements.

As associations seek opportunities for nondues revenues, "partnering" arrangements, such as affinity programs that allow members to purchase various products or services, often at a special association member discount, have appeal. As associations expand into these types of deals on the Internet, the typical contract will establish that the association must prominently place the other organization's logo at its Web site. Careful planning is needed to establish a framework for placement of these third-party logos. Some organizations may specify that their logo must be placed "above the fold"—visible to visitors at the association's home page, without the need to scroll down. These are elements to consider in contractual negotiations. Careful coordination may be needed to avoid entering into multiple contractual agreements that ultimately include inconsistent provisions or requirements that become infeasible to implement based on prior agreements.

---

[9] *See Intellectual Reserve, Inc. v. Utah Lighthouse Ministry, Inc.*, 75 F. Supp. 2d 1290 (D.Utah 1999).

D. Copyright Basics

For many, copyright is one of the murkiest of the IP issues. The widespread notion that once something is placed on the World Wide Web it is "free" has led to even more confusion about copyright on the Internet. Content is key to building traffic on the Internet—the all-important "stickiness" that is the *sine qua non* of a successful site. Copyright is critical, then, to the Internet, and copyright issues are raised in connection with the software that you use to make your site available, as well as to the text, images, and sound on your site.

1. Copyrightable Works and Rights of Authors

Copyright protects *"original works of authorship."*[10] Associations are both creators and users of copyrightable material. Newsletters, reports to your members, statistical compilations, conference proceedings, and even ad copy can be copyrightable. Computer software, photographs, videos, and artwork are also copyrightable. Copyright is distinguished from trademarks in that trademarks identify the source or origin of products. Trademarks seldom show the requisite originality to be subject to copyright protection, absent a significant design component. Copyrights are also different from patents, which are designed to protect novel inventions or processes.

Copyright owners have the exclusive right to do (or to authorize): (1) copying, (2) distribution, (3) display, and (4) public performances (in the case of musical, dramatic, literary, choreographic, motion pictures, and similar audiovisual works) of copyrighted works. Visual artists have some special additional rights. At one point, copyright owners who failed to display the notice of copyright on a work lost their copyright rights, but that is no longer the case. Nevertheless, adoption of copyright notices may deter infringement and also preclude an infringer from raising an "innocent infringement" defense in the event of litigation. Thus, associations should include a copyright notice on their Web site that complies with the requirements of the Copyright Act. This means that notice should include: (1) the copyright symbol (©), the word "Copyright," or the abbreviation "Copr."; (2) the date (year) of first publication; and (3) the name of the copyright owner. The phrase "All rights reserved" or "All rights reserved in any medium now known or later invented" is often added as well.

Copyright is said to "subsist" or begin the moment an original work of authorship is "fixed" in any tangible medium of expression. In other words, when pen or brush is put to paper, copyright exists. Copyright is limited in duration, but protection exists for the life of the author plus 50 years (in the case of an individual author), for 75 years from first publication (in the case of a work for

---

[10]17 USC § 101 *et seq.*

hire), or for 100 years from the date of creation, whichever comes first. In contrast, trademark rights are perpetual so long as the mark is used. Patent protection is limited, usually to 20 years from the filing date of the patent application.

One aspect of copyright law important to Web site operators is the potential that sites offering chat rooms or other opportunities for public postings could face liability if a visitor infringes on someone else's copyright. The Digital Millennium Copyright Act[11] includes a safe harbor provision to avoid potential copyright liability for third-party content.

2. "Works for Hire"

Copyright issues are most commonly raised in the Internet arena because of the widespread use of consultants and other third parties to provide content (including computer software). Although copyright law establishes that an original work created by an employee within the scope of his or her employment is a "work for hire," copyrighted to the employer, the law is different for independent contractors. In those instances, a work is only a "work for hire" if it falls within a certain category of specially commissioned work *and* there is a written agreement between the parties that the work is a "work for hire."[12] *All agreements with third parties creating content for your site should include a work for hire/copyright assignment provision to protect your rights.* This includes Web development firms, advertising firms, and/or interactive agencies. These agreements should mandate that all subcontractors to your consultants must also enter into specific work for hire/assignment agreements, and include language specifically waiving any "moral rights" the actual author may have in the work as well. And remember, this issue affects contributions by your members as well. Often, associations run into problems not just with consultants or third parties, but when a "volunteer" decides that he or she should be paid for a contribution or can use the contribution independently of the organization. This can compromise association programs like testing, educational, training, or certification programs if it occurs.

Another wrinkle on the work for hire issues involves traditional publications that the association now wishes to make available via its Web site. A recent ruling of the United States Supreme Court dramatically illustrates the importance of obtaining copyright rights for materials posted online.[13] A number of freelance authors challenged actions by The New York Times, Newsday, Inc., and Time, Inc., related to articles that they had previously contributed to copyrighted "collective

---

[11]Pub. L. No. 105–304, 112 Stat. 2860, signed into law Oct. 28, 1998; codified at 17 U.S.C. §§ 101, 104 *et seq.*

[12]Works for hire include specially commissioned works, developed pursuant to a written agreement signed by both parties establishing that the work is for hire and falling into the following categories: 1. a contribution; 2. part of a motion picture or other audiovisual work; 3. a translation; 4. a supplementary work; 5. a compilation; 6. an instructional text; 7. a test; 8. answer material for a test; or 9. an atlas.

[13]*New York Times Co. et al. v. Tasini et al.*, No. 00201. Argued March 28, 2001. Decided June 25, 2001.

works" published by these publishers. Actions included licensing the articles to electronic database publisher LexisNexus, among others. The publishers argued that they were merely republishing articles that had been previously published in collective works. The freelance writers, in contrast, argued that the electronic republication allowed the collective work copyright holders, namely, the publishers, to exploit their articles beyond the scope of the revision privilege authorized under the Copyright Act. In a seven to two ruling, however, the Supreme Court sided with the authors.

The decision turns on nuances of Section 201(c) of the Copyright Act. This section establishes that copyright in an article contributed to a collective work vests initially in its author, but allows entities like The New York Times, an association, or another entity to claim copyright in the "collective work" in which the individual article appears. Section 201(c) also allows the collective work copyright holder to revise the collective work; this is the basis on which the publishers claimed their actions were protected from liability under the Copyright Act. The Supreme Court rejected the publisher's claim of privilege, saying that the 201(c) privilege to revise a collective work did not override the author's copyrights. The databases did not reproduce and distribute the articles as part of a collective work privileged by 201(c). In short, the fact that the electronic medium allowed for individual articles to be searched and viewed was an important factor in the Court's decision.

This decision is of seminal importance to anyone interested in Web publication. It may ultimately have a bearing on an association's ability to post conference proceedings/papers and similar collective works online in an individually searchable format. *Tasini* illustrates just how essential it is to obtain broad copyright rights, at least on a going forward basis.

Your work for hire/assignment agreements should specify that rights include all copyright rights to do or to authorize publication, display, reproduction, performance, translation, and the like, in any medium whatsoever now known or later developed throughout the universe, without the need for any additional licenses from or payments to the author.

Additionally, it occasionally happens that companies with whom you are negotiating Internet deals attempt to claim rights under copyright law that they really are not entitled to claim. For example, remember that copyright does not protect ideas, processes, methods, or principles, but only creative works of authorship "fixed" in any tangible medium. Software is copyrightable, for example, but a method or process for "remembering" a customer's Internet order is not (although it may be patentable). Make sure that your agreements properly reflect the IP rights that you, your consultants, and your business partners have.

3. Obtaining Rights to Copyrighted Works

The flip side of the copyright question involves the need to obtain ownership or license rights to the IP of others posted on your Web site or IP (like software) used to make your site available. As noted previously, this could include content developed by members (perhaps including pictures). Model releases will also be needed if you post pictures of identifiable individuals. Associations may also want to consider adding language to their membership forms stating that any work they do for the association is considered a "work for hire" (or that copyrights are assigned to the association), and any copyrightable material they author for the association is owned by the association.

Another attractive aspect of the Internet is the opportunity it offers for distance learning, alone or in combination with other technologies, like satellite broadcasts. As more associations seek to develop relationships with educational institutions, seek grants for government funding of education and training programs, and consider how to utilize these distance learning technologies, establishing copyright ownership and license rights becomes key to structuring the arrangements. Although developing cooperative arrangements with outside parties to provide content and assist in educational efforts makes sense, clear contractual provisions on IP rights are essential.

As technology advances, and Web sites seek to become jazzier, associations also face questions about negotiating rights in some less familiar territory—audio and video. Just as you must obtain special rights and develop special agreements to deal with association-sponsored videos or film, so, too, do you need to consider these issues on the Internet. Their use may necessitate negotiations with the various artists' guilds, an area totally unfamiliar to most associations. With streaming video and audio feeds becoming a reality, however, this will fast become a point on which associations must be knowledgeable. Recently, for example, the Copyright Office dealt a blow to broadcasters in ruling their licenses only covered "over-the-air" broadcasts and not "digital audio transmissions."[14] Although negotiations with performing artists are underway, rights issues remain unsettled.

4. Digital Millennium Copyright Act

Congress enacted the Digital Millennium Copyright Act[15] (DMCA) to implement two World Intellectual Property Organization (WIPO) treaties and to address other significant copyright issues. Although the DMCA includes many complex provisions, the most important of these for associations is Title II, the

---

[14]The rule amends 37 CFR § 201.35(b)(2).
[15]Pub. L. No. 105–304, 112 Stat. 2860 (Oct. 28, 1998).

Online Copyright Infringement Liability Limitation Act. Title II adds a new Section 512 to the Copyright Act. It limits the liability of "online service providers" for copyright infringement when engaging in certain types of activities important in the digital environment. The categories of conduct by a service provider include: (1) transitory communications, (2) system caching, (3) storage of information on systems or networks at the direction of users, and (4) information location tools.

Importantly, the Act defines a "service provider" differently for different exemptions. The "transitory communication" exemption is defined in a manner that may limit its application to true Internet Service Providers (ISPs) and providers of backbone telecommunications services. For purposes of the other exemptions, a "service provider" is "a provider of online services or network access, or the operator of facilities therefore." Thus, it may offer protection for associations.

To qualify for the limits on liability, which include a complete bar on monetary damages and restrictions on the availability of injunctive relief, a service provider must adopt and implement a policy of terminating the accounts of "subscribers" who are repeat infringers and must accommodate and not interfere with "standard technical measures" adopted by copyright owners to protect their works. This will be most relevant to associations that offer chat rooms, bulletin boards, and other features where members or others can post potentially infringing materials. Other provisions specify that a service provider is not obligated to monitor its service or access material in violation of a privacy law (like applicable wiretapping provisions) to be eligible for the liability limitations.

Other provisions of the DMCA will be of interest to a smaller universe of nonprofit organizations. The DMCA establishes special provisions governing the liability of nonprofit educational institutions based on the actions or knowledge of a faculty member or student employee performing teaching or research at the institution. Again, slightly different rules apply depending on the particular limitation involved. For limitations on liability for transitory communications or system caching, the faculty member or student teacher is deemed a "person other than the provider." For the other limitations of liability under the DMCA, the knowledge of the faculty member or student teacher will not be attributed to the educational institution when the following conditions are met: (1) the infringing activities do not involve providing online access to course materials that were required or recommended during the past three years; (2) the institution has not received more than two notifications over the past three years that the faculty member or student teacher was infringing; and (3) the institution provides all of its users with informational materials describing and promoting compliance with copyright law.

The DMCA also amends section 108 of the Copyright Act to permit libraries and archives to make up to three copies of a copyrighted work that is damaged, lost, or deteriorating, or if the format that the work is stored in becomes obsolete. These copies now may be digital, but digital copies may not be made available to the public outside of library premises.

E. Patents

Patents give their owners a legal "monopoly" to the covered invention for up to 20 years[16], and the prospect of generating licensing revenues is a major consideration for patent-holders. Most associations have typically had few concerns about patents, but in the e-environment, business process patents are increasingly important. For example, Amazon.com's "one-click" ordering method and Priceline.com's reverse auctioning processes are the subjects of patent litigation. As a practical matter, associations must establish contractually that: (1) the firms helping them set up their operations have appropriate rights to practice the technologies associated with their e-commerce activities, (2) the rights are licensed to the association, and (3) the licensor will hold you harmless in the event of infringement litigation. This is essential, as litigation for alleged infringement of business process patents is one of the fastest-growing areas of IP infringement.

Unlike many businesses, associations have traditionally not been concerned about the possibility of their employees developing inventions of potential value. As a preventive measure, however, associations should consider including in employee handbooks requirements that inventions developed in the course of an employee's work for the association are the property of the association. Specific provisions on inventions and discoveries should also be included in employment agreements, if those are used, and consideration should be given to establishing such agreements with key employees.

F. Trade Secrets and Confidential Business Information

Trade associations are accustomed to handling confidential information in the context of statistical and other programs. Confidentiality issues can be implicated in a variety of ways in the e-commerce environment. Initially, exploratory discussions with e-business service providers are often done under general confidentiality agreements, usually drafted by them and often overbroad—in their favor. These sorts of agreements should be scrutinized carefully to make sure they do not unduly impede your ability to obtain requests for proposals from other providers and the like. Similarly, you may be sharing confidential information about your computer networks and systems, your membership, your databases, and other aspects of your operation when you deal with net providers, even at a very preliminary stage. Confidentiality agreements must be mutual, and should

---

[16]35 USC § 154(a)(2).

include nondisclosure and possibly even noncompete provisions to protect the association and its members.

One of the most critical issues is to establish your ownership rights over member information, visitor clickstream data, and so forth. Much of this data will never qualify for other types of IP protection, so it is important to safeguard it carefully to protect your organization. Maintaining appropriate firewalls and security mechanisms to safeguard data, as well as establishing access limits (*e.g.,* password-protected access to some types of data) are essential. If you allow members and visitors to make purchases at the site, appropriate security for credit card information is also a must. Security measures (like adoption of "Secure Sockets Layer" [SSL] technology) are standard for the transmission of credit card data. Maintaining appropriate internal security to limit employee access to credit card numbers, encryption, and the like may also be needed. A growing number of firms are specializing in data security measures, and outsourcing your database management for this type of sensitive data may be useful, with appropriate warranties, assurances, and hold harmless agreements.

A related but sometimes overlooked issue is the extent to which your own employees and any consultants working on database management and Internet issues may have essential business information that will be difficult—and possibly expensive—to duplicate. Processes which require employees (or consultants) to document hardware and software "fixes" are one way to make a parting of the ways, if one occurs, a bit easier for the organization and can be outlined in an employee handbook. This, however, requires consistent management oversight to make sure the tasks are being performed as required. Another is the use of employment contracts that specify required practices and include confidentiality and noncompete provisions.

G. Valuing Association Intellectual Capital

Associations and other businesses sometimes fail to aggressively protect their IP for two reasons: (1) they may not always fully understand the differences between the various types of IP, and (2) they lack the tools to fully understand the value of their IP. As a practical matter, different valuation methods may apply to different types of IP. The publications an association offers are relatively easy to value, as the value is based on the net expected revenues—sales minus total costs to produce.

It is harder to put a price on the value of more intangible IP, like an association's trademarks and know-how. Yet, associations offer personal contacts, name recognition through their organizational names, trademarks and logos, and may have a significant amount of information that can be considered the association's trade secret information. Even if that knowledge falls outside of traditional IP categories, it reflects a tremendous amount of knowledge and skill which is often hard to quantify but difficult, time-consuming, and potentially costly for someone else to duplicate. Associations, therefore, can and should try to value their "intellectual capital" because this is a critical element of any negotiating strategy in entering into a B2B agreement with a for-profit corporation.

For example, an association endorsement can aid a B2B venture in obtaining start-up or additional capital, meaning that the right to use the association's name alone can be of considerable dollar value. The association's ability to introduce a business partner to the right decision maker at a member company is another example of what the association brings to the table. Finding the right balance between overestimating the value of your IP and underestimating it is an important but little understood task. In a recent *Smart Business for the New Economy* article, the author discusses the inability of normal accounting methods to value intellectual capital: "We're talking about the worth of the intellectual capital—intangibles like people, ideas, reputations, relationships, and legally protected intellectual property."[17] As a result, the associations that protect and promote the value of their intellectual capital will be in a better bargaining position.

---

[17]"Money From Nothing," Don Steinberg, *Ziff Davis Smart Business for the New Economy*, April 2001.

III. INTERNET AGREEMENTS

A host of agreements of varied complexity and importance are involved in making a Web site available, with even more complex agreements associated with setting up or "endorsing" B2B ventures. The key to any successful contract arrangement is mutuality. That means that the association must identify its primary objectives, as well as the objectives of the other party, establishing arrangements that both feel are mutually beneficial. Depending on the complexity of the arrangement (*e.g.*, a B2B negotiation), a step-wise approach using multiple and increasingly more definitive contractual instruments is not only useful, but it is often inevitable.

A. Web Hosting, Maintenance, Development, and Related Contracts

Once you have established a domain name, you are ready to start the Web site. Associations are immediately faced with a variety of questions about the structure of their Web offerings. Typically, Web hosts are used, with the host company taking on all or many of the technical maintenance obligations associated with the site. Depending on the level of sophistication of in-house staff, companies may contract with third-party Web developers, which might be advertising agencies and/or specialized interactive companies, or other consulting firms. The selection of the right consultants depends on the level of technical sophistication and content desired at the site. Whatever the approach, a series of contractual agreements will be needed. Virtually every agreement will have to address a range of IP protection questions.

To help you sort out hosting, maintenance, and development responsibilities, you should either provide to prospective consultants (or ask consultants to provide to you) a request for proposal (RFP), or at least develop a checklist of the fundamental requirements for your Web site. Your RFP should include a basic description of your Web site objectives, and establish that the information you provide to the consultant(s) is confidential or proprietary. Ask for URLs of Web sites that the consultant has worked on, and check references. Ask for a breakdown of fees to separate Web development fees from hosting and maintenance fees, and make sure both parties understand who will provide and "own" content.

Whether you or your ISP/consultant will host the site, you must immediately address what operating system(s) will be used and what compatibility issues are raised for your members and visitors as a result. Initial decisions need to be made on whether you will primarily offer text, or will include complicated graphics or streaming audio or video. Assuring that your visitors will have a consistent experience using different browsers and platforms is typically desired. You should identify the hardware and software necessary to make the site available as part of the specifications, and pay particular attention to "site critical" elements. Most associations offer public as well as member-only areas. Some offer special subscription services geared to members or nonmembers. Some offer e-mail updates with links to new features or content on the Web site. These features must be built into the design, and programming costs to provide these features should be covered in the contract.

Web hosting agreements may vary in complexity, but some agreements are actually surprisingly favorable to the Web site. They may include specific provisions that require quick responses (with a turnaround time of no more than a few hours) to fix technical problems, specify that routine maintenance will be done only in off hours (*e.g.*, between 2 a.m. and 3 a.m.) or preclude scheduled maintenance during normal business hours (*e.g.*, between 7 a.m. and 7 p.m., EST), and establish technical backup criteria for saving data. Warranties that the server will be kept up to date are needed and should include provisions obligating the host (or developer) to apply available software patches and/or upgrades. Agreements should address security issues and establish what, if any, rights employees of the Web site, as well as your employees, may have to access the server for various purposes. Processes to handle viruses, hacking, and other security problems should be set out so that both parties are clear on responsibilities.

As noted previously, a central consideration for Web development and hosting agreements is the issue of IP, particularly copyright ownership of content and software used to make the site available to your members, consumers, and other visitors to your site. It is essential to address copyright rights to materials developed for your Web site by third parties, and ownership/licensing rights to software used or developed. This means that contracts must incorporate copyright work for hire and assignment language, mandating that independent contractors working for the developer also sign similar agreements.

Obtaining ownership or license rights to software is another important issue. The developer should identify all hardware and software (both third-party off-the-shelf as well as proprietary software) that will be used to make the site available. The agreement should establish appropriate license arrangements for third-party and proprietary software and requirements that the developer identify all software used and update the list periodically. In theory, you will be able to readily obtain rights to off the shelf software if you need to terminate an agreement with the developer or host, as long as you can identify it. If possible, you should negotiate for ownership of proprietary software, or at least a perpetual, royalty-free license to use it (with any modifications tailored to your site). Failure to get those rights could either lock you in to the developer, or require you to start from scratch if you choose another provider, possibly even requiring you to take down your site for a period of time. The goal is to assist you in seamlessly recreating the site should you have a parting of the ways with your Web site developer. Warranties of noninfringement of copyright, patent, and other rights should be provided by the developer, along with hold harmless provisions in the event of violations. Remember that those who themselves are only licensees of software or other IP rights will usually provide warranties limited to their "knowledge, information and belief" that the intellectual property is noninfringing.

The design or "look and feel" of your site is really part of your organizational identity. This may mean that you want your home page to include items consistent with a major publication your members are familiar with. Your agreements should establish requirements (and time frames) for the Web developer to provide you not only with the technical specifications for the site, but also with a site map that illustrates how the site will be navigated. Timing and payment milestones should be established, linked to approval mechanisms set forth in the agreement.

Remember that timing also depends on association approval schedules. Experienced Web site developers may try to include provisions specifying that payment schedules will not be delayed because of lagging association approvals, or specify that materials are deemed approved within a set period of time unless disapproved by the client. These provisions can actually be useful to associations in forcing often complex and cumbersome committee structures to act promptly. Establishment of a "shadow" site can be an important feature that allows for a preview of the site before it goes live. Sometimes associations and the developer find that operating under a "silence is acquiescence" rule may help both sides keep the project on track, forcing the association to provide timely feedback on aspects of the site.

The parties involved in the site must establish a thorough understanding of data ownership from a privacy perspective, and the site owner should identify a contact to handle inquiries about privacy at the site if personally identifiable information (PII) will be collected. And a process for modifications to the site must be established. You should control the content and be able to prohibit unauthorized material or modifications to your site. Some Web consultants may propose language specifying that they will have exclusive rights to all digitized content on the site; such provisions should always be rejected, for that means you are essentially ceding your Web site content to a third party.

Acceptance and testing procedures are an essential part of an effective legal risk management strategy which must be included in Web site development agreements to assure that you are ultimately in control of content at your site. Provisions establishing an approval process before the site goes live may be supplemented with provisions that include additional responsibilities to correct "bugs" that may arise when the site is publicly available.

Although everyone hopes that these agreements will result in the successful launch or revision of a Web site, termination provisions are essential to protect the site. Often there is a great deal of subjectivity in determining when a site is acceptable. Your image and reputation, and that of your entire membership, are at stake, however, and it should be solely within your discretion (consistent with reasonable commercial practice) to determine this. That means that termination provisions should allow for termination if the site is not acceptable. They should also allow for immediate termination in the event of breach, such as a breach of confidentiality, failure to honor confidentiality provisions, failure to keep current the list of hardware and software, and failure to follow approval mechanisms before posting content. Of course, confidentiality, security, and noncompete/nonsolicitation provisions are essential. User/visitor data should explicitly be yours.

B. E-Commerce Agreements

Adding an e-commerce component to an association site can add layers of complexity to contracts. Your actual offerings on the Web may be based on a variety of models. You may offer members or others an opportunity to register for association events, conferences, or trade shows, or to buy products or services online. Some associations are experimenting with banner ads. Some offer special subscription areas. Some develop "partnering" arrangements with third parties for e-commerce sales of products and services like insurance, office supplies, and employment assistance reflected in Web distribution-types of agreements. Some offer "buying clubs" (which may be subject to state regulations). Other types of agreements are affiliation-types of arrangements, which may involve linkage to an e-commerce site, endorsement of the e-commerce opportunities at a third party site, shared content, and various types of payment options for hits, leads, advertising revenues, and e-commerce sales.

Complicated issues of pre-existing business relationships between the site and your members may need to be addressed. Thus, in addition to agreements related to Web posting, Web maintenance, Web and content development, a variety of e-business agreements may be involved in a nonprofit organization's site. Web linking agreements, advertising agreements, co-branding, and co-marketing agreements are only some of the other agreements that may be involved.

The complexity of many e-commerce arrangements often requires a step-wise approach to the negotiation. For many dot-coms, their negotiating position will be driven by advancing investment and liquidity goals. These are obviously key to assuring the long-term success of an e-venture. But making sure that you agree on how the arrangement will advance your member services goals (and reserving the right to withdraw if it does not) is key.

At the initial stages of discussion about an e-commerce arrangement, a short nondisclosure agreement might be needed. Careful attention is required to the specific content of such agreements before signing. Often they are broadly drafted to establish that all information shared is deemed confidential, subject to only specific narrow exclusions (like information already in the public domain). They may preclude not only disclosure to third parties but also "use" of any information disclosed during the discussion for a period of time, sometimes several years. Use limitations have very different ramifications in the association world, because associations are rarely going to "use," in the sense of practicing it, disclosed technology. "Use" of information, without disclosing it, can be an element of negotiation with others. For example, you may technically "use" information about a potential business partner's discount policy in attempting to negotiate similar (or better) rates with someone else, even if you do not disclose their rates to the other party. Thus, limits on use may effectively restrict even discussions with other potential business partners. Those types of provisions are generally overbroad and should be rejected in favor of much more narrowly crafted provisions more suitable for the type of operations of most associations.

Exclusivity requirements as well as noncompete provisions are often components of e-agreements. Associations should approach exclusivity carefully, particularly arrangements involving members. Associations, like other businesses, should be free to make appropriate business arrangements with vendors and others on whatever terms and conditions seem reasonable. Some antitrust review may be needed to establish that association exclusive arrangements can be justified, however.

As discussions progress, it may also be helpful to first establish an agreed-upon list of "principles" to use as a guiding document in further contract negotiations. This may help in ultimately crafting a Memorandum of Understanding (MOU) or even a Definitive Agreement to govern the e-commerce arrangement.

E-commerce arrangements may often involve delicate negotiations about payment, where valuing the contributions of the respective parties is a major issue. IP valuations are difficult in the best of circumstances. In cooperative arrangements where the association and the other party are typically both contributing in-kind services and products to the deal, valuation becomes even more complicated. This is particularly true because often the association contributes zero hard cash. It is not atypical for e-commerce businesses to value their in-kind contributions at a higher level than those of the association, sometimes using measures like lost billing revenues instead of a straightforward calculation of time, salary and benefits, costs and overhead. Make sure you inquire about valuation measures and push for "apples to apples" approaches from a fairness standpoint.

Often, e-commerce businesses are paying for your association's endorsement, so the contractual arrangement ultimately is akin to a trademark licensing or affinity agreement. Sometimes agreements specify that the association must offer a certain amount of advertising and marketing support, must provide personnel to assist with taking orders, must cooperate in promotional seminars, must rent member lists, and/or must offer free or discounted space at conferences and trade shows. These added costs should be factored into the association's calculations. And, to the extent the association commits to facilitating personal introductions with key members, this "door-opening" opportunity can save the e-commerce partner significant sums in its own initial start-up marketing efforts. This is another element to consider in coming up with a fair compensation scheme.

Consider arrangements that provide for an annual, semi-annual, or quarterly royalty or sponsorship payments for the use of your name and trademarks, royalty or other payments for hits attributable to your association's promotional efforts, and/or percentages of e-commerce revenues (including sales and advertising). Equitable stakes are also options that some associations may find appealing (but may be even more complex to negotiate). Combination approaches are also possible. Tax planning can be a critical element of these arrangements.

Ownership of content on and information generated from the site is key. The World Wide Web is not dissimilar from television in that sites generating revenues, in whole or in part, from advertising, are actually in the business of selling "eyeballs" to advertisers, using their content to attract visitors. Most sites relying on advertising revenue simply share anonymous, aggregate data with their advertisers. But many Internet companies seek access to specific user or subscriber information as part of the agreement, and will use, rent, or sell the personal information involved (even if it is only names, addresses, and e-mail addresses) to other parties for direct marketing purposes. Privacy and security issues are raised by many of these agreements, particularly if you plan to accept credit card information online and the site is under the control of the association.

Another issue that arises in connection with online sales or advertising on an association site is the question of the association's potential liability for any endorsement it offers to a B2B business partner. If member companies advertise on either the association's site, or an e-commerce business partner's site, and a purchaser is unhappy, what are the implications for the organization? Associations which accept advertising on their site should consider adopting advertising guidelines or advertiser agreements. Your e-contracts should specify the association's position on endorsements and specify that the site does not endorse the products or services of advertisers. Member relations issues may suggest that other rules are desirable in connection with advertising.

Associations must decide on the method by which sales will occur. Will you simply post a member directory or guide? Will you offer (with or without a fee) links to member sites? Will you allow advertisers to post a classified ad (with or without click-through opportunities)? Will you simply offer an online mall with posted prices and sell directly through the association Web site? Will you offer only a supplier's guide or directory? Will you cooperate by endorsing an independent exchange hosted by a third party? Will the exchange offer opportunities for a type of peer review to be posted on the products and services available online? If you are offering (or promoting) a B2B exchange, what model is being used (auction, reverse auction, closed auction, group buying, bartering, open bid, closed bid, pre-qualification of buyer or sellers, etc.)? Disclaimers suitable for these various approaches may be needed, even after an antitrust and liability review establishes that the proposed activity is legally appropriate.

Often, however, fulfillment services for product delivery are made available through outside parties. Sites may offer "facilitation" services to customers, but shipping, credit card processing, and other services may be provided by other entities. Again, negotiating ownership of and access to data is a key concern, and establishing discount policies for members where applicable, and payment terms to the third parties need to be addressed contractually. Sales issues may be even more complex on B2B sites. You will want to establish authorization mechanisms to determine when employees of your members may make purchases at your site, establish specific credit limits for individual employees or companies, and adopt policies to govern other similar issues.

C. Other Contracts

Advertising, linking, and co-branding agreements are also common on the Internet. Business models for such arrangements—and consequently contracts governing them—vary widely. Elements of a trademark license agreement are almost always involved. Ownership and control of user data is typically an essential element, implicating privacy and confidentiality issues (and potentially antitrust issues) for associations. The standard approach of a "cost per million" model for advertising (the advertiser pays for the number of "eyeballs" or "clicks") may often be unsuited for association sites, which may have smaller and very targeted audiences. The very nature of the targeted opportunities associations offer through their defined membership, however, should be worth considerably more to the right business partner. Revenue-sharing arrangements, flat fees, or lead fees (you get paid for the number of leads you provide the advertiser) are among some of the alternatives. Simple sponsorship arrangements are also potentially involved.

Associations must also be aware that moving certain activities to the online world may require wholesale changes to old, standard agreements geared to online activities. Statistical reporting is an example. Traditionally, associations have often dealt with third-party fiduciaries to manage confidential statistical reporting programs. Sometimes, the fiduciaries offer proprietary software that they license to the association. Web-based programs may change this, allowing elimination of old provisions prohibiting reverse engineering of the consultant's software because the software may not reside on the association's server, so it is not accessible to association personnel. With this model of statistical reporting, the traditional agreement with your fiduciary must be expanded to include Web hosting and maintenance responsibilities. Access rights, security, and confidentiality of data must be addressed.

Another new value-added aspect with statistical reporting is the potential ability to negotiate access to data about transactions occurring on sites operated by e-business partners (consistent with your general antitrust guidelines for your statistical programs). These data may be used to establish trends, to provide independent confirmation of other statistical data the association collects, or for other legitimate reasons. Careful coordination with counsel on aspects of access to individual transaction data, however, is crucial for antitrust compliance purposes.

Downloadable diagnostic types of offerings made available to members through your Web site are another case in point. The contract with the software owner should include appropriate indemnification provisions, and disclaimers of liability for the association. (These disclaimers should of course be repeated at the site.)

D. Web Site Terms of Use

Most commercial U.S. Web sites post a user agreement, terms of service, or terms of use that provides information on the activities of the site, disclaimers of liability, and other important information. Associations have traditionally paid little attention to user agreements, but they can be a vital part of your overall risk management strategy. Specific "as is" language to address hacking, viruses, and limits on site availability is essential, along with disclaimers of responsibility for the content of linked sites, or of information provided by advertisers or other third parties (if any). Debates continue about whether these should take a "click to acknowledge" form, "pop-up" when a visitor enters, or are simply provided via a link somewhere on the home page, but most sites continue to use the link method.

IV. ANTITRUST CONSIDERATIONS

Real excitement exists about the B2B opportunities of the Internet, and a number of industry associations (and ad hoc groups of competitors) are evaluating ways to allow members to buy and/or sell products online. This has led to concerns about the potential for B2B sites to engage in conduct that violates the antitrust laws. In April 2000, the Federal Trade Commission (FTC) and the Department of Justice (DOJ) issued their *Antitrust Guidelines for Collaborations Among Competitors.*[18] It provides an analytical framework for examining the organization and operation of B2B sites. The FTC and DOJ also hosted a workshop on antitrust issues of B2B during the summer of 2000, reflecting the increased interest that regulatory authorities and industry have on the topic. That workshop resulted in a FTC report titled "Entering the 21st Century: Competition Policy In the World of B2B Electronic Market Places"[19]. A second workshop was held in May 2001. In the absence of blatantly illegal conduct, such as price fixing, the competition authorities and the courts should seek to determine whether the procompetitive advantages of the collaboration outweigh any anticompetitive harm from the collaboration, using these existing guidelines. This has generally been the approach followed by the regulatory authorities.

Although Internet transactions and B2B sites are based on new or emerging technology, the same fundamental analytical framework continues to apply. The essential question is: How is

---

[18]Released April 7, 2000.
[19]Oct. 2000 Staff Report, http://www.ftc.gov/os/2000/10/b2breport.pdf.

competition affected? In other words, the courts and enforcement officials will speculate on how the market will function with or without the particular B2B site in question and determine whether its functioning was anticompetitive based on an overall analysis. As a practical matter, enforcement officials or a private company seeking to challenge the operation of a B2B site would initially determine whether any facially illegal activity has occurred such as fixing prices or production, or allocating territories, customers, or markets. Assuming that no facially illegal activity occurred, the competition analysis might be restated as determining whether the procompetitive advantages outweigh any anticompetitive harm from the collaboration. In either case, however, the analysis is complicated by the reality that the Internet offers instant information opportunities, which can be communicated worldwide with the click of a mouse. Whether that constitutes the effective functioning of Adam Smith's perfect marketplace or collusive violation of antitrust laws remains to be seen, and will likely differ in particular cases.

Based on the Guidelines noted above, associations and their members can look at nine basic questions to assess the legality of Internet and e-commerce conduct under U.S. antitrust laws.

1. Does the B2B Internet site operate as an unadorned agreement to fix prices, curtail output, or divide markets?

2. Does the B2B site set standards that are anticompetitive?

3. Is the site an essential business facility?

4. Does the site create significant barriers to entry for new participants or significant barriers of entry to Internet transactions by existing competitors?

5. Does the site create anticompetitive network effects?

6. Does the site create a monopoly or a monopsony?

7. Does the site facilitate inappropriate information exchange?

8. Does the site have auction functions that operate in an anticompetitive manner?

9. From an analytical perspective, should Internet sites be treated like retail and other marketing formats that help define the product market?

The structural organization and ability of various participants to access certain types of market information may well be crucial factors in this regard. Is the site limited to individual seller and purchase agreements, or does it involve collective buying? (Collective buying is clearly legal, but antitrust concerns may arise when the market is very concentrated or when the cooperative buying accounts for the lion's share of the market.) Is participation available on nondiscriminatory terms using software and connection standards that are readily available when the Internet site serves as a market or purchasing vehicle? Are there capacity-related purchasing or selling requirements, such as requiring 10% or 90% of a company's sales or purchases in the relevant product market to be made through the site? Can participants float proposed, future prices in an effort to learn the reactions of their competitors? Positive answers to these questions may make it more likely that a site crosses the line.

In addition to these nine broad issues, there are additional factors that an antitrust analysis should consider. These include consideration of current or historical market practices, the overall competitive profile of the industry, and the relationship to and impact on traditional offline sales and distribution channels. The real challenge is to determine what characteristics B2B sites have that distinguish them from traditional markets. The most frequently mentioned aspect is the speed of information exchanges among large groups of people. Within this context, conduct that may not have been troublesome in more traditional market settings may create anticompetitive effects in the Internet setting. On the other hand, information distribution and competitor coordination that may have been suspect in traditional markets may have a procompetitive effect in the Internet setting.

Associations engaged in B2B activities—whether as site operators or as market participants—will want to be sure to closely evaluate the competitive implications on their industry, on their members, and on the market as a whole. For associations being asked to endorse a particular B2B venture, the question of exclusivity may be raised. Associations, like other businesses, are typically free to enter into appropriate business arrangements on an exclusive basis. But requiring members to use the B2B as an exclusive provider may present a very different antitrust question. Particularly in the face of information suggesting that both buyers and sellers prefer neutral marketplaces, such arrangements may present practical business problems in generating participation.

Antitrust concerns are also potentially posed by unmoderated association chat rooms or bulletin boards. Members may have an opportunity to improperly discuss pricing, capacity, or other forbidden topics. It is prudent to provide a mechanism to register chat room or bulletin board participants (most organizations prefer to limit this "benefit" to members only). As an adjunct to registration, consider offering a link to the association's antitrust rules (and other rules on use of appropriate language, etc.) in association chat entry areas, using a "click to acknowledge" feature prior to entry or upon registration.

Associations must also remain keenly aware that their antitrust responsibilities do not change when they move certain activities, like statistical reporting, online. The same rules that govern the appropriateness of a particular industry statistical-reporting program offline (like the minimum number of participants, maximum percent market share that any one participant may hold, prohibition on direct sharing of data, etc.) are equally valid online. And, maintaining confidentiality of individual data on sales and the like is crucial. Online statistical-reporting mechanisms can be devised to properly protect confidentiality. Indeed, access to certain information generated by a B2B site, like trend data, may enhance competitiveness and reduce costs when collected, aggregated, and reported as part of the association's normal statistical-reporting program.

V. PRIVACY

Privacy has become one of the most talked-about issues of the Internet. Development of new technologies that allow for more (and sometimes surreptitious) collection of information has fueled debate about whether an overarching law on privacy is needed in the United States. Visitors are asked to provide PII to register at a Web site, to sign up for e-mail lists, to make purchases, and sometimes to receive information. In addition, tracking technologies are available to monitor visits, often allowing the Web surfer to be tracked across multiple Web sites and allowing for online profiling. Some information is collected automatically, like the type of browser the visitor uses, so that the technological environment can be optimized for the consumer. Fears that these anonymous data will be linked to PII have created some level of general suspicion about the Internet. Companies concerned that this will halt the growth of e-commerce have developed various types of self-regulatory programs and guidelines on privacy as a result.

This can affect associations in several ways. First, nonprofit organizations may collect and use information from members of the public. This is especially true for arts and cultural organizations, and educational institutions. Even associations that collect personal information only from business members, however, are dealing with individuals. Antitrust considerations as much as privacy considerations suggest the need for caution in sharing certain types of personal (or even company-identifiable) data, particularly if the association offers e-commerce purchasing or selling opportunities to members. And, many e-commerce and other business partners will require access to association member data as part of the arrangement for direct marketing purposes. Consequently, privacy considerations will become increasingly important to associations.

A. U.S. Privacy Law and Principles

Privacy is a complex topic. Some countries or regions, like the European Union (EU) and Canada, have chosen to adopt broad, general laws on privacy. The United States, however, has opted for a different approach. A rather elaborate series of sectoral privacy regulations have been adopted in the United States to govern activities like wiretapping, telecommunications activities, credit, and, more recently, collection and use of financial and health care information. The United States also adopted a special law, the Children's Online Privacy Protection Act (COPPA)[20], which became effective in April 2000, when the FTC issued implementing regulations.[21] COPPA requires *"commercial Web sites"* to obtain *verifiable parental consent* from parents before collecting and using personal information from children under age 13. To date, however, there are no general laws in the United States specifically addressing Internet privacy. Moreover, the fact that COPPA covers only commercial Web sites should exclude most nonprofit organizations from its reach. Nevertheless, 7,000 bills on privacy have been introduced at the state level, and more than 300 bills at the federal level. Whether or not federal privacy legislation is enacted, there is broad recognition that all Web sites should address privacy. Consequently, it is only sensible for nonprofit associations to consider privacy.

The U.S. government has largely supported a general reliance on self-regulation, with specific legislation enacted as needed to address specific privacy concerns related to certain types of data (like health or financial data), or specific practices (like wiretapping) of concern. From the standpoint of marketing data (exclusive of sensitive financial or health data), industry and government representatives generally agree that privacy protection should focus on the following core "Fair Information Practice Principles" (FIPPS)[22]:

1. **Notice:** Web sites should provide *clear* and *conspicuous notice* of their data collection practices. This includes information on the *identity* of the Web site operator or data collector; *how* information will be collected (passively or voluntarily); *uses* for collected PII; whether PII will be *shared* with third parties (which may include affiliates), and, if it is shared, the *types of third parties* with

---

[20]Title XIII of the Omnibus Consolidated & Emergency Supplemental Appropriations Act, Pub. L. No. 105–277, 112 Stat. 2681, signed Oct. 21, 1998, and codified at 15 U.S.C. § 6501 *et seq.*

[21]Children's Online Privacy Protection Rule, 65 Fed. Reg 59887–59915 (Nov. 3, 1999), effective April 21, 2000, 16 CFR Section 312.

[22]Fair Information Practice Principles, first articulated in the U.S. Dept. of Health & Human Services' 1973 Report, *Records, Computers and the Rights of Citizens, See also OECD Guidelines on the Protection of Privacy and Transborder Data Flows of Personal Data* (1980); Federal Trade Commission, *Fair Information Practice Principles,* June 4, 1998, http://ftc.gov. reports/ privacy3/fairinfo.htm.

whom it may be shared. More recently, notice concerns have focused on whether certain types of passively collected data (*i.e.*, data collected through cookies) might be linked with PII to create a profile of the individual.

2. **Choice:** Consumers should have an opportunity to consent to the collection of PII, and to prevent further uses (like sales of their name or profile information to a third party unrelated to fulfilling a requested transaction).

3. **Access:** Consumers should have a means of determining exactly what information an operator has about them, and a right to contest the accuracy, update, change or request deletion.

4. **Security:** The integrity of data should be protected.

The regulatory authorities have added a fifth element: **Enforcement.** Regulatory authorities believe that a mechanism to assure that privacy protections are in place should be established.[23]

Associations should consider the privacy issue in the context of their own activities. Because of the importance of this topic, and concern that failure of self-regulation will lead to onerous regulations in the United States, many associations are also encouraging their members to adopt and adhere to a privacy policy at their own Web sites. Some associations are also offering assistance to members in setting up privacy policies in member Web sites. Most associations that do tend to offer guidelines rather than attempting to draft privacy policies for their members. Policies should be tailored to the information collection activities and offerings of each site.

B. International Privacy Issues

I. EU Data Directive

The EU Data Directive[24], adopted in 1995, took effect in October 1998. The Directive begins with the premise that data should be collected for specific, legitimate purposes, and not processed in a manner incompatible with that purpose. Privacy in the EU is treated as a fundamental human right. In the United States, while privacy is a highly important (and, depending on the circumstances, constitutionally protected) right, the U. S. system strongly relies on notice and choice elements to allow *consumers* to decide when, and under what circumstances, to share data. The Data Directive is not limited to data collected online and covers employee data collection, use, and transfer. Associations operating internationally should review it from a broader perspective.

---

[23]The Federal Trade Commission (FTC) has filed a number of enforcement actions for privacy violations, many relating to misrepresentations about privacy practices. State Attorneys General have as well. Private lawsuits, including class action suits, have also been filed citing a variety of theories and laws. Use of cookies and other passive tracking devices and attempts to sell data in violation of a posted privacy policy have triggered legal actions.

[24]Directive 95/46/EC of 24 October 1995, Official Journal of the European Communities, No. 281/31.

There are several key differences between the U.S. approach and the EU approach to privacy. First, implementing regulations must be adopted in each European country, and this process is not yet complete. The Data Directive includes elements like "limiting purpose" and "limiting use." The U.S. approach has been to focus primarily on the notice element to advise consumers of why data are being collected and how they are being used, allowing the consumer to then choose whether or not to provide PII. The EU Data Directive includes provisions that assure that data are up-to-date, and kept in a form that allows identification of the data subject for no longer than necessary. The Directive does not distinguish between children and adults. Although certain self-regulatory codes relied upon internationally, like the International Chamber of Commerce's Guidelines for Advertising and Marketing on the Internet, recommend that Web sites make a reasonable effort to obtain parental consent before collecting data from a child, there are no special legal rules in place to protect children's privacy in the EU; their data are covered under the Directive.

Another key difference is that the right of privacy in the United States must always be balanced against the First Amendment. Journalistic exceptions appear rather restricted under the Directive. A feature of the EU Data Directive is its conferral of authority on national "Data Protection Authorities" (DPAs), the regulatory bodies within each country charged with protecting privacy. The EU Data Directive does not establish an EU-wide DPA. Privacy advocates in the United States have been lobbying for establishment of a privacy regulatory body in the United States, but opposition, on fiscal and other grounds, exists in the United States to the creation of a new government agency or body.

Directive 95/46 prohibits transfers of data to countries that lack an "adequate" privacy regime. The U.S. approach is to focus on notice to allow consumers to choose when, and under what circumstances, to share PII, regardless of the location of the recipient, and to promote self-regulation, regulating on a sectoral basis as needed. Critics argue that the EU may attempt to target U.S. organizations. However, lax enforcement within the EU has been the norm to date. Although actions have been initiated against several countries that have failed to adopt implementing legislation, there have been no private enforcement actions against EU companies for violations of the Data Directive.

2. Canada's Personal Information Protection and Electronic Documents Act

Canada has now adopted a general privacy law.[25] The Canadian law is based on self-regulatory guidelines developed by the Canadian Standards Association, which in turn derive from the EU Data Directive. It therefore includes provisions

---

[25]Personal Information Protection and Electronic Documents Act, Royal Assent received April 13, 2000. May be found at http://www.privcom.ge.ca/english/102_06_e.htm.

on data transfers between provinces and out of Canada, similar to the EU's provisions barring data transfers to countries lacking an "adequate" regime to protect privacy. While the requirements will be phased in over time, provisions barring interprovincial and international transfers by certain entities went into effect January 1, 2001. The law is based on ten principles. They are:

1. Accountability (by the data collector)

2. Identifying purpose (notice)

3. Consent

4. Limiting collection

5. Limiting use, disclosure, and retention

6. Accuracy

7. Safeguards

8. Openness

9. Individual access

10. Challenging compliance

Like the EU Data Directive, the Canadian privacy law differs from the U.S. approach. Since, in the wake of the North American Free Trade Agreement (NAFTA), more associations are considering organizing on a "North American" basis, as many of their members do, the Canadian law could have a more significant practical effect on both the Internet and non-Internet portions of associations than even the EU Data Directive.

The Canadian privacy law includes some important specific restrictions, like a requirement that companies appoint an individual responsible for privacy, as well as mandatory time frames for responses to consumer access requests. It also relies on an "openness" principle that mandates that a company's policy and procedures on privacy be made readily available. This does not necessarily require that the entire policy be posted on a Web site, but supplementing information must be provided. There is also some debate about whether consent to provide data must be provided in an "opt-in" or "opt-out" mode. Although the law itself appears to acknowledge that opt-out may be appropriate, officials within the Privacy Commission have expressed reservation as to the use, for example, of pre-checked boxes that sign consumers up for e-mail mailing lists. These requirements should be factored into an organization's overall privacy policy.

C. Practical Tips on Online Privacy

Privacy, of course, is a concern in the offline world, and there are employment-related privacy issues that associations must contend with as well. Nevertheless, the Internet has crystallized public concerns about the issue. Associations may partner with third-party firms to offer online shopping and other features that require the collection of personal data from members of the public as well as association members, and potentially collection or sharing of that data with your third-party contractors. And, even where you use a Web host to actually run your online operation, it is the Web site's sponsor whose credibility is at stake. Associations should never simply copy another firm's privacy policy. Privacy policies should be developed so that they reflect your data collection practices. In doing so, you will want to consider the following tips on structuring privacy policies:

> Involve your key employees in developing your privacy policy. Make sure your consultants and your business partners understand your wishes regarding collection and use of PII, particularly third-party sharing.

> Posted privacy policies should summarize what kind of personal and non-personal information is collected, the general reasons why it is collected, and how it might be used (including if it will be sold to or shared with third parties). If you have concerns that your visitors might respond adversely to these disclosures, then you might want to reconsider the reason for collecting the information.

> Make sure your contracts with Web hosts, data management firms, ad server companies, contest firms (if applicable), and so forth, address privacy.

> Explain what information is gathered automatically (like IP addresses, etc.) and how you use cookies, Web beacons, and other features. Cookies, for example, allow the site to "remember" a password or set up an account.

> Identify the site "operator(s)" (who collects data at the site).

> Disclose whether information is shared with any third parties, and whether shared data consist only of anonymous, aggregate information or include PII. This becomes an important aspect depending on e-commerce, linking, and similar agreements.

> Describe why you require information that you collect (*e.g.*, a home address is essential to allow you to ship products ordered online by a member or consumer). If the information will also be used by the association or one of its business partners to market or promote their products or services to the individual, that should be indicated as well.

> Your privacy policy should establish that if a visitor chooses to share PII in chat rooms or bulletin boards, it is available for anyone to use. Reinforce this (and your antitrust rules) in chat room rules.

> Provide opt-out and unsubscribe options for web visitors. Consider opt-in if you collect sensitive data, like health or financial data.

> Your policy should specify that your site has no responsibility or authority over linked sites, unless you link only to sites under your direct control which operate with an identical privacy policy.

➤ Include specific language reserving the right to use or disclose information as required by law, to maintain site security, or to respond to legal process (*e.g.*, a warrant or subpoena).

➤ Your link to your privacy policy should be clear and prominent, using techniques like size, contrasting color, and so forth, to make sure it is visible to your visitors.

➤ Try to minimize legal jargon and avoid inconsistent statements. Question and answer formats may be helpful in presenting information in a consumer-friendly manner. Charts may also be helpful.

The privacy debate will likely continue, as it is one that consistently rates high on consumer polls indicating concern about the Internet. Notices about privacy practices should help demystify this important area, and enhance confidence in your site.

D. "Spam"

Spam is generally considered to be "bulk" e-mail messages from companies advertising goods or services that the Internet user did not ask to hear about. Anti-spam legislation has been enacted in a number of states, and federal legislation is pending before the U.S. Congress[26]. Some industry members support federal legislation as a way to avoid a patchwork of inconsistent state laws. The tension here is between the First Amendment right to communicate and the right of individuals to be left alone, leading many in the United States to focus on the use of opt-out registries as a way of handling the issues. For associations, bulk e-mails may be a convenient way to let people know about conferences and events, particularly if they are open to the public or to nonmembers. Using common sense in sending e-mails and offering unsubscribe options should alleviate most concerns for typical association activities.

Some state spam laws, to avoid some of the First Amendment issues, offer specific exceptions for associations to communicate with their members. Nevertheless, spam laws should be considered in the context of deals where you grant business partners access, for marketing purposes, to information about your members or others. Among the features of some proposed federal anti-spam bills, are requirements that unsolicited e-mail messages include an accurate return address and be labeled as an advertisement. These are features of many state laws, which also require that senders enable recipients to opt-out of receiving unsolicited messages. State attorneys general have also been interested in the spam debate. They

---

[26]See, e.g. H.R. 718, *The Unsolicited Commercial E-Mail Act of 2001*. Introduced by Rep. Heather Wilson (R-NM), HR 718 was reported out of the Energy & Commerce Committee April 4, 2001. H.Rept. No. 107–41, Part I. See also, S.630, *Controlling the Assault of Non-Solicited Pornography and Marketing Act of 2001*, introduced by Sen. Conrad Burns (R-MT).

are urging that federal legislation grant them enforcement authority, including authority to bring class action suits.

Additionally, unsolicited commercial communications are an issue of concern in the EU. A proposed directive would require companies to obtain opt-in consent before sending unsolicited commercial communications by e-mail (or other new communications techniques).

VI. ONLINE SWEEPSTAKES AND CONTESTS

One of the fastest areas of growth on the Internet involves contests, sweepstakes, and gaming. Some associations have offered member-only contests offline (for example, contests with prizes awarded to those who bring in the most new members). Apart from general restrictions on lotteries, gambling, and so forth, many of the laws on contests and sweepstakes will arguably not apply to member-only contests, as they are not offered to consumers. Some nonprofit organizations, however, sponsor public contests and sweepstakes for prospective members or consumers and would be subject to the various federal, state, and, unless carefully constructed, international laws governing consumer sweepstakes and contests.

When conducted in a purely traditional manner, contests and sweepstakes subject their sponsors to a host of state and federal laws and regulations, to say nothing of the myriad of foreign requirements. In general, the requirements offline are well understood. Although it may sometimes be cumbersome, sponsors of contests and sweepstakes in the United States have been able to structure sweepstakes and contests using disclaimers and well-crafted contest rules to avoid running afoul of specific state laws. The design and formulation of an Internet sweepstakes or contest promotion, however, requires care and specialized knowledge of all the regulatory challenges to limit legal exposure.

Four federal agencies (the Department of Justice, the U.S. Postal Service, the Federal Trade Commission, and the Federal Communications Commission) enforce federal laws that specifically apply to sweepstakes, primarily related to illegal lotteries. All fifty states have statutes that prohibit illegal lotteries, many of which differ markedly from each other, making compliance difficult. In addition, states may regulate sweepstakes directed to consumers depending on the value of the prizes. Some states require sponsors to post bonds (*e.g.*, New York and Florida require registration when the total value of prizes exceeds $5,000); and some require pre-registration (*e.g.*, Arizona requires registration of all intellectual contests; New York and Florida do when the total value of prizes exceeds $5,000; and Rhode Island does for retail promotions when the total value of the prizes exceeds $500). Many states require the sponsor to provide specific disclosures in specified font types in immediate proximity to a sweepstakes headline, and some require disclosures on a sweepstakes envelope sent via the mail. Requirements of offline (mail) promotions must be considered because promotions are often both mailed to prospects directly and posted online.

Liability does not end at the U.S. borders. Because the Internet is global, promoters also are required to comply with the laws of foreign countries. Belgium, Malaysia, and Norway prohibit sweepstakes. France, Hong Kong, and Spain require registration, fees, or governmental approval. Others, such as Italy and the Philippines, require a local drawing. Some countries require sweepstakes to be conducted in the local language. Canada, notably in Quebec, has laws that differ significantly from those of the United States.

What is the difference between a legal sweepstakes and an illegal lottery? An illegal lottery is characterized by three elements, all of which must be present: (1) a prize, (2) chance, and (3) consideration. If one of these elements is eliminated, an illegal lottery is transformed into a legal sweepstakes. Eliminating "consideration"—providing anything of value to participate in the sweepstakes—is the method sponsors generally employ to avoid conducting illegal lotteries. (Eliminating the element of chance creates a game of skill or a contest as opposed to a lottery.) Traditionally, sponsors have eliminated consideration by simply stating no purchase necessary, and offering a free method of alternative entry, such as mailing in a postcard.

The nature of the Internet and the means by which individuals access it complicate the issue of consideration. Consideration may be anything of value, even the increased time it takes a person to enter the sweepstakes, if the difference is found to be significant. And, with new attention to privacy, how PII generated from a sweepstakes may be used is another important issue. Care must be taken in contest or sweepstakes rules to include disclaimer language for problems in accessing networks, and to specify that those eligible must already have access to the Internet on the entry date (to avoid a consideration problem). Other technical rules abound. Suffice it to say that for associations considering sweepstakes or contests as fundraising mechanisms, particularly when they are offered to consumers, advice of expert counsel is a must to avoid liability.

VII. LIABILITY PREVENTION

Associations usually provide information and services to members. Many associations develop standards and offer accreditation and certification services. Occasionally, however, associations are drawn into litigation based on allegations that they somehow owe a duty to warn, to inform, and/or to protect members of the public from hazards about industry products or activities. The cases, while fortunately rare, may involve industry standards or certification activities, "guidelines" or recommendations on how to use products or services, or performance claims about products or services of members. Common-sense rules applied to offline activities should also be applied to online activities to limit and manage your liability exposure in these areas. In addition, associations must be aware of new potential areas for liability exposure that their Internet activities may involve.

A. Claims, Advertising, and Links

As with your association written materials, videos, and so forth, associations must take reasonable precautions to ensure that information available to the public on their Web sites about products and services of the organization and the industry is accurate and not misleading.[27] Make sure that you can substantiate claims. This may mean not just relying on a representation by

---

[27]Section 5(a)(1) and (a)(2) of the FTC Act, 15 U.S.C. §§ 41 *et seq.*, establishes the Federal Trade Commission's (FTC) general authority for false advertising. Trade associations have been found to be subject to FTC jurisdiction. See, e.g., *National Commission on Egg Nutrition.* 88 F.T.C. 89, aff'd, 570 F. 2d 157 (7ᵗʰ Cir.), *cert. denied*, 439 U.S. 821, *reissued*, 92 F.T.C. 848 (1978).

a member, but actually gathering technical and other information that supports the statement. Use care in describing the benefits of your industry products or services, and pay particular attention to how you advertise or promote your standards and certification or accreditation programs.

Another potential liability consideration involves claims made by members or others at sites linked to the association's site, or in banner ads posted at your site. Traditionally, disclaimers are used to limit liability. Disclaimers on your Web site should make clear that by offering links to other Web sites you are not endorsing the products and services of members or other third parties. Disclaimer provisions should be included in your terms of use or user agreement posted at the site. Disclaimers (*e.g.*, at member directory areas where you offer links to member sites) should be repeated. Relatively simple language can be used, such as:

[Association] provides links for the convenience of its members and visitors. [Association] is not responsible for content at linked sites, and does not endorse or recommend the proprietary products or services offered at any linked site.

Contracts are a key liability-limiting tool. They must be carefully drafted and include appropriate warranties and hold harmless agreements to protect you. Also, associations should consider adopting standard linking agreements if they allow members or others to link to the association site. Linking agreements are really a form of trademark license agreement. They allow an association to keep track of the use of its mark on a member's or another's Web sites. Linking agreements do not have to impose a fee, although they can be a source of licensing revenue while limiting liability. Provisions can include termination clauses for inappropriate use (such as use in a manner which implies an endorsement, violation of placement or size limits, etc.) and include hold harmless provisions for the association.

B. Chat Rooms, Bulletin Boards, and "Ask an Expert" Areas

In addition, the Internet poses new challenges where bulletin boards and chat rooms are concerned, and not just on the antitrust front. The World Wide Web provides an opportunity for individuals around the world to express themselves and to try to create communities of individuals with similar views or interests. In the process, however, new liability concerns are presented.

These concerns take several forms. First, Web site operators fear liability for comments posted online by visitors. Libel and defamation, and possibly even tortious interference with contracts, are some of the types of claims that might be raised. As noted above, chat rooms and bulletin boards may also offer opportunities for members or others to engage in information exchanges of a type prohibited under the antitrust laws. Second, associations may offer an "ask the experts" area where recommendations on products, installations and other items are provided.

Similarly, recommendations and advice on a host of issues are typical in chat rooms and bulletin boards, or through posting of association documents and publications. This category of activity can raise product liability questions for the association. Third, the availability of the Internet (and of e-mail) has led to new liability issues for employers.

To some degree, using filtering technologies that filter out sexually explicit material and offensive words may help minimize the potentially offensive aspect of chat room discussions. But filters may not be 100% effective, and certainly can't address the untoward remark about prices or capacity, the negative statements about the fact that a member (or another third party) failed to deliver products or services or has quality deficiencies, or an inaccurate recommendation. User agreements, terms of use or terms of service, and special chat room rules, coupled with activity-specific disclaimers at the site, offer reasonable approaches to minimize the association's liability for Web site activities. That is why a "click to agree" feature which necessitates that visitors to your chat room or bulletin board rules acknowledge and agree to those rules can be an important liability-limiting approach for associations. Chat room rules can also be part of or incorporated by reference into a posted "user agreement" at the site which outlines the terms and conditions for use of the site, and those terms and conditions can be incorporated by reference into the chat room rules. Similarly, the association's antitrust guidelines can be part of the chat room rules. Of course, where issues or problems are brought to the association's attention, prompt action is nevertheless desirable to address any issues raised.

Associations should also be aware that they may obtain some protection under Section 230 of the Communications Decency Act (CDA).[28] The CDA was primarily enacted to protect children from indecent and pornographic materials available on the Internet. Much of the CDA was found to be unconstitutional in a seminal case[29] that concluded that the Internet, as a medium, should be accorded the highest standard of First Amendment Protection. Section 230 of the Act, however, provides a provider or user of an interactive computer service with "Good Samaritan" protection. In essence, Section 230 establishes that "No provider or user of an interactive computer service shall be treated as the publisher or speaker of any information provided by another information content provider." The first decided case under Section 230 exonerated AOL from liability for defamation claims involving the Drudge report.[30] In general, while there may be limits on the scope of this protection, particularly relative to intellectual property infringement

---

[28]47 U.S.C. §230.

[29]*Reno v. American Civil Liberties Union*, 521 U.S. 844 (1997). Similar provisions of a successor law, the Children's Online Protection Act (COPA)—not to be confused with the Children's Online Privacy Protection Act (COPPA) - were also found to be unconstitutional. *American Civil Liberties Union v. Reno*, 217 F. 3d 162 (3d Cir. 2000), *petition for cert. filed* (No. 00–1293), February 26, 2001.

[30]*Blumenthal v. Drudge*, 992 F. Supp.44 (D.D.C. 1998). *See also Ben Ezra, Weinstein and Co. v. America Online, Inc.,* 206 F. 3d 980 (10th Cir. 2000), *cert. denied* 121 S. Ct. 69 (Oct. 2, 2000). *But see Gucci America v. Hall and Assoc.,* 135 F. Supp. 2d 409 (S.D.N.Y. 2001) (Mindspring not immune under §230 for claim of trademark infringement based on hosting of infringing site).

claims, associations that make a good faith effort to eliminate objectionable material from their Web site should be able to claim protection under Section 230 from defamation and other tort claims.

C. Security–Confidentiality, Hacking, Viruses, and Denial of Service Attacks

Hacking is a growing concern, along with what are called "denial of service" attacks. Your site and your databases should include filters, firewalls, and other standard mechanisms to protect the integrity of information. Many associations use third-party providers to collect and manage statistical data and do not maintain individual company data in their databases. Nevertheless, statistical data is an area of special concern. Similarly, organizations that offer employee or member certification or accreditation programs will want to be particularly careful about maintaining secure databases for test questions and answers to assure the integrity of the testing program. Sometimes contracting for database management services becomes the most cost-effective way to address security and integrity concerns. Agreements can include appropriate provisions on firewalls and state of the art security, as well as hold harmless and indemnification provisions.

The transmission of computer viruses is another potential issue. The Melissa virus that affected hundreds of thousands of businesses last year spread through user groups and listservers (both government and private). Firewalls and virus scanning software are business necessities in today's environment. This includes making these tools available for association employees who are increasingly using laptops to conduct association business.

D. Insurance

Another element of risk management planning is insurance. Unfortunately, traditional insurance policies may be inadequate to deal with the type of "business interruption" you may suffer from a hacking incident, from the inadvertent transmission of a computer virus to others, or from the inadvertent disclosure of confidential information. Many association insurance policies do not cover antitrust liability (but may cover defense costs), and the shape of certain B2B ventures may create a significant alteration in how an insurer would view the organization's antitrust exposure. There is a real need for evaluation of the scope of your insurance coverage in a changed environment.

E. Consumer Fairness

The Internet also gives nonprofit organizations the option to allow members of the public to purchase certain products or services online. Colleges and universities, museums, school associations, consumer and environmental groups, and arts organizations, have developed online shopping opportunities for members of the public to purchase products and services online. Trade associations rarely do so. The quality of the products, warranties provided, shipping and return policies, and a host of other issues are raised by online sales to consumers. Moreover, a variety of self-regulatory initiatives are under development to help consumers feel confident about their online transactions, recognizing that consumers are concerned about security, and product integrity.

Associations are typically well aware that their value depends on the strength of their brand but may have only limited experience in consumer sales. They may contract e-commerce activities at their Web site to a third party, and contracts should require that the site's policies and procedures adhere to all relevant consumer laws. The FTC has developed a useful publication, *Electronic Commerce, Selling Internationally*,[31] which includes some practical tips on steps to enhance consumer confidence online. Web sites dealing with consumers should:

➤ Use *fair* business, advertising, and marketing practices.

➤ Provide *accurate, clear,* and *easily accessible information* about the company and the goods or services it offers.

➤ Disclose full information about the *terms, conditions,* and *costs* of the transaction.

➤ Ensure that consumers know they are making a commitment to buy before closing the deal.

➤ Provide an easy-to-use and secure method for online payments.

➤ Protect consumer *privacy* during electronic commerce transactions.

➤ Address *consumer complaints* and difficulties.

➤ Adopt fair, effective, and easy-to-understand *self-regulatory policies* and procedures.

➤ Help *educate consumers* about electronic commerce.

Many U.S. Web sites have already instituted these recommendations in their sites.

Just as with for-profit companies, your brands—your association's name and logo—are among your most valuable assets. Offering quality products and services, making sure that terms, conditions, and costs are clear to purchasers, addressing returns and warranties, and having knowledgeable representatives to answer questions are among a Web site's most effective tools in handling consumer complaints and protecting their trademarks.

Finally, e-discovery is a growing issue. We all have read about the comments made in e-mails by Bill Gates in connection with the Microsoft antitrust suit by the Department of Justice. Consider this in the context of association meetings. Your members appear at a meeting, many of them with laptops. Some of those members will have their own version of events and activities that occurred during

---

[31]Issued March 2000. It can be found at http://www.ftc.gov/bcp/conline/pubs/alerts/ecombalrt.htm

the association meeting e-mailed almost before the end of the meeting. Discrepancies between various member versions and the official association minutes can create questions in the event of litigation. Similarly, a host of questions arise regarding how to document transactions and events on your Web site, particularly where you are offering online sales opportunities, "ask an expert" areas, and similar offerings in the e-environment. Saving data to disks, printing out versions and saving them, and dating updates are some of the possible options. Considering electronic documents in the context of your records retention policies is important because discovery requests routinely now demand access to electronic records (including back-up tapes) in many instances. You should note that e-mailed documents were electronically generated and simultaneously retain hard copy versions, especially for documents such as minutes.

VIII.
EMPLOYMENT ISSUES

Associations, like any business organization, must consider the employee aspects of the Internet and their e-mail systems very carefully. Improper use of electronic systems should be addressed in employee handbooks and training programs. It is vital to understand the potential issues posed by electronic communications, which may be governed by a diverse array of laws.

A. Employment Agreements

Employment agreements, including employee noncompete, confidentiality, and IP ownership clauses, are becoming more commonplace in today's transient marketplace. Many companies are looking to employment agreements to protect their valuable technologies, trade relationships, and trade secrets, such as client lists and business methods. It may be difficult for associations with limited resources to focus on comprehensive programs for employee agreements, but they can be extremely valuable in offering protection of your confidential information.

In general, employment agreements provide the terms of the work relationship and often include provisions restricting the use of proprietary information when the employee leaves the company. Confidentiality clauses in employment agreements protect valuable information such as member lists, technologies, business methods, data, documents, and contemplated products or services. In addition, noncompete clauses within employment agreements can protect member and employee relationships by prohibiting an employee from working for a member company for a period of time. These agreements can also protect proprietary Information Technologies (IT) used by the association; in fact, with the growing importance of technology for associations, IT employees are a good place to begin implementing this policy. However, these types of agreements must be drafted carefully to provide appropriate protection for the employer without depriving the employee of opportunities to work elsewhere.

For many years, and to some extent today, employment agreements containing noncompete clauses were frowned upon by the courts. Additionally, state laws on the subject vary and many states prohibit these agreements for professionals. In general, laws limit the protections afforded companies to a specific time period (usually 1–2 years) and limit protection to a very specific geographic region. Further, while confidentiality clauses are not traditionally frowned upon, they must be drafted carefully in order to provide the greatest protection for the company.

Another important aspect of an employment agreement is the establishment of company ownership of all IP developed by the employee during his or her tenure. Historically important to for-profit businesses, whose employees could develop potentially patentable inventions during the employee's tenure, patents have been of limited concern to most associations not engaged in research and development efforts. With the growth of business process patents, however, more firms are considering the issue. If employees develop potentially patentable information, such an agreement could prevent future disputes about patent ownership. If deemed suitable for your association, the agreement should include provisions requiring the employee to assist in any filings with the Patent and Trademark Office and assignments or licenses of the IP by the organization.

Employment agreements can be used most effectively as part of an overall employee management plan and protect the valuable information and skills gleaned by employees during their tenure with you. This is especially important in the research and development or new technology development department of an organization, including a nonprofit organization, where employees have access to IP. It is best to present an employment agreement at the start of employment or during some watershed event, such as an annual review or new position and/or raise. Additionally, the employment agreement should contain termination provisions and survival provisions requiring the employee to abide by the terms (especially the confidentiality provisions) for a specified period after the employee leaves the company. Stipulated damages clauses may also be helpful in the event of breach by the employee because it is often difficult to place a dollar value on the information protect by the breached agreement.

B. Wiretapping and Surveillance

Several U.S. laws address privacy and integrity of communications in a way that may affect certain employment activities. The Electronic Communications Privacy Act of 1986[32] (ECPA) governs privacy of wire, electronic, and oral communications "affecting interstate or foreign commerce." Telephone and voice mail systems, as well as e-mail communications, fall under the ECPA. Title I of the Act prohibits the intentional interception of such communications and the use or disclosure of information known to be obtained through the illegal interception of the communication. Title II is designed to prevent hackers from obtaining, altering, or destroying certain stored electronic communications. The Federal Wiretap Act[33] and Computer Fraud and Abuse Act[34] are also relevant. State laws also exist.

In general, existing U.S. laws do not preclude necessary monitoring by associations or other employers. Laws have been introduced, however, to require that employees be given notice of electronic surveillance. The Notice of Electronic Monitoring Act,[35] introduced in July 2000, would have required employers to inform employees in writing that they are being monitored. This type of legislation could resurface. The EU Data Directive and the Canadian Privacy Act, among other laws, do cover collection use and transfer of certain employee data. Associations operating internationally should be sure to check applicable local law in their country of operation to be sure that their policies on employee data collection (including surveillance, storage, transfer, and use) comply.

C. Discrimination and Harassment and ADA

A number of cases have been brought seeking to impose liability on employers for creating a hostile workplace environment based on employees who e-mail jokes, allowing pornographic images to be viewed by fellow-employees, and similar actions. In a recent New Jersey case, a female pilot successfully sued Continental Airlines after complaining of sexual harassment through allegedly pornographic and vulgar comments posted about her on a bulletin board extranet open to Continental employees. Dow Chemical fired a number of employees who were found to have been involved in sharing and accessing pornographic materials on their company computers; other employees were suspended or disciplined. It is vital that associations follow up on any complaints of improper content (sexually explicit images, jokes, derogatory comments, etc.) involving your e-mail system or

---

[32]18 U.S.C. §2510 *et seq.*
[33]The Federal Wiretap Act is Title One of the Electronic Communications Privacy Act.
[34]Pub. L. No. 99–474, 100 Stat. 1213, signed Oct. 16, 1986, 18 U.S.C. § 1030 *et seq.*
[35]H.R. 4908, introduced by Rep. Schumer (D-NY), July 20, 2000.

your Web site by your employees. Similarly, you should investigate complaints related to action or conduct by employees of your members.

Employees should be made aware that their use of your internal e-mail system and network creates a trail of electronic paper that can result in your ability to identify offending communications and the senders and recipients of those communications. Attempts by the employee to use passwords or to delete information may be ineffective because the association can often locate information on backup systems. Moreover, if a sexually explicit, racially charged, or threatening communication is deleted by the employee, the recipients may print and save copies themselves as evidence of improper action.

IX. WEB ACCESSIBILITY

A newer aspect of the Internet which will likely increase in importance relates to accessibility to persons with disabilities. The U.S. Department of Commerce's (DOC) National Telecommunications and Information Administration (NTIA) Access Board has issued proposed standards on the accessibility of government Web sites to persons with disabilities under Section 508 of the Rehabilitation Act.[36] The law applies to all Federal agencies when they develop, procure, maintain, or use electronic and information technology. Federal agencies must ensure that electronic and information technology is accessible to employees and the public. A final rule implementing these requirements took effect June 21, 2001.[37] Although they will apply only to government Web sites, the initiative, begun during the Clinton Administration, is part of a movement to make sure that electronic communications are more broadly accessible to persons with disabilities. The World Wide Web Consortium (W3C) has developed Web Accessibility Guidelines that address what makes Web sites accessible to persons with disabilities. Certain types of audio and video formats may not be readily adaptable to accessibility requirements.

---

[36]Pub. L. No. 99–508, 100 Stat. 1848., signed Oct. 21, 1986.
[37]Architectural and Transportation Barriers Compliance Board, "Electronic and Information Technology Accessibility Standards," 65 Fed. Reg. 80499 (December 21, 2000).

X. JURISDICTION

When an organization is on the Web, whether it is a for-profit or a nonprofit organization, it is global. Anyone who has a computer with access to the Internet can find you, whether he or she is in Antarctica, Austria, the United States, or the United Kingdom. In a medium that can be accessed from virtually anywhere in the world, the key question is determining what laws apply to the operation of your Web site, and the transactions initiated through your site. These questions must be answered for every facet of your operations, particularly if you are involved in e-commerce. It is particularly crucial for nonprofit organizations whose scarce resources make the expense of dealing with litigation in a distant jurisdiction especially burdensome. Because e-commerce is more advanced here than elsewhere in the world, the United States has had a few years of experience within which cases have been brought and decisions have been made relevant to jurisdiction.

Web site-related case law in the United States has focused on issues of *personal jurisdiction*: whether and when a particular Web site's presence and activity subjects the Web site operator to the authority of a particular court in a particular state. (Questions about courts' *subject matter jurisdiction* or *choice of law* as they relate to Internet transactions have not been widely reported, nor have any of the reported cases to date involved nonprofit organizations.) The law in the United States on the exercise of specific personal jurisdiction based on a defendant's Internet activities is still just developing. The courts have had to adapt traditional minimum contacts analysis to the new phenomenon of globally accessible Web sites. The most common approach to measuring contacts, beginning with the case of *Zippo Manufacturing Co. v. Zippo Dot-Com, Inc.,*[38] has been to analyze the nature and quality of *commercial activity* that an entity conducts over the Internet, applying a sliding scale. This may ultimately be an important issue that distinguishes many association sites from commercial sites.

At one end of the scale—where personal jurisdiction is improper—is the passive Web site. "A passive Web site that does little more than make information available to those who are interested in it is not grounds for the exercise of personal jurisdiction."[39] Thus, when a New Jersey woman tried to sue an Italian hotel chain in New Jersey after she had been a guest and fallen at one its hotels in Italy, personal jurisdiction on the basis of the hotel chain's presence on the Internet was not found. The hotel's Web site merely advertised its services by providing photos of hotel rooms, descriptions of hotel facilities, and telephone numbers required to establish general personal jurisdiction.[40] The association site that simply offers general information to the public should not find that this action expands its liability from a litigation standpoint.

At the other end of the sliding scale are highly interactive sites on which an entity conducts substantial, possibly high-volume business, including the formation of contracts. *Zippo* itself is a case in point. There, the Pennsylvania maker of "Zippo" cigarette lighters succeeded in establishing personal jurisdiction in a trademark infringement suit brought in Pennsylvania against a California corporation that operated a Web site with the domain name of "zippo.com." On its Web site, the California company advertised an Internet news service to subscribers. Three thousand Pennsylvanians applied and paid for subscriptions on the Web site to the Internet news service. The company had also contracted with seven Internet service providers in Pennsylvania to permit subscribers to access the news service. The court concluded that Dot-com had "purposely availed" itself of doing business in Pennsylvania.[41]

In the middle of the scale and more difficult for the courts to decide are cases in which defendants maintain Web sites that allow users to exchange information with a host computer. Here "the exercise of jurisdiction is determined by the level interactivity and commercial nature of the exchange of information that occurs on the Web site."[42]

The thorny nature of jurisdictional issues is illustrated by a controversial decision last fall by a French court requiring Yahoo! Inc., to block access by French Web surfers to its U.S. site because that site offered neo-Nazi memorabilia for sale, a violation of French law. The French court determined that it had jurisdiction

---

[38]952 F. Supp. 1119 (W.D. Pa. 1997).
[39]*Zippo*, 952 F. Supp. at 1124.
[40]*Weber v. Jolly Hotels*, 977 F. Supp. 327, 333–34 (D.N.J., 1997).
[41]*Zippo*, 952 F. Supp. at 1125–1127.
[42]*Zippo*, 952 F. Supp. at 1124.

over the U.S. site because it was easily accessible to French citizens, made even more accessible due to links on the Yahoo! French site that allowed the French visitor to directly access the U.S. site. Yahoo in turn filed suit in California, seeking a declaratory judgment by the U.S. District Court for the Northern District of California that the order of the French court was unenforceable and violated its First Amendment rights. A nonprofit group, La Ligue Contre le Racisme et l'Anitisemitisme, and others, asserted that the California court lacked jurisdiction over them in the dispute, and sought dismissal on jurisdictional grounds. The court disagreed, ruling that it did have personal jurisdiction over the foreign nonprofit entities in the matter.[43]

The Court ruled that it could exercise specific personal jurisdiction over the foreign nonprofit defendants because (1) the defendants purposefully availed themselves of the privilege of conducting activities in the United States, thereby invoking the protection of U.S. laws; (2) the plaintiff's claim arose out of the defendants' activities in the forum; and (3) the exercise of jurisdiction was reasonable.

In applying the "purposeful availment" test, the Court was persuaded by the fact that the defendants deliberately accessed the Yahoo! Web site in the United States, directed a cease and desist letter to Yahoo! at its California headquarters, asked the French courts to require Yahoo! to initiate specific remedial actions in California on the Yahoo! server to block access to the site by French citizens, and used U.S. Marshalls to serve Yahoo! with their suit. The fact that the French decision impinged on constitutionally protected rights of a U.S. company was another factor, as was the U.S. court's special expertise in interpreting matters of U.S. constitutional law. The Court noted that the global nature of the Internet enables people around the world to "virtually" visit almost any site, regardless of its location. To permit the French nonprofit organization to seek enforcement of the order in France could result in any provider of Internet content being subject to legal action in countries that might limit freedom of speech and expression in a manner repugnant under U.S. law.

The Court was further persuaded that advanced communications systems meant that the French nonprofit defendants would not suffer undue hardship by being required to litigate the case in California, particularly in light of the interest (and expertise) of U.S. courts in making legal determinations on constitutional issues.

Associations, like most Web sites, increasingly desire to interact with their customers. To date, the question of how an association site which offers "members-only" chat areas, accepts limited advertising in public areas, and/or offers online sales of its technical literature to the public at large at its site fit within the *Zippo*

---

[43]*Yahoo! Inc. v. La Ligue Contre le Racisme et l'Antisemitisme et al.*, No. 00-21275JF, June 7, 2001.

sliding scale analysis has not been addressed, but the legal implications of these different levels of interactivity should be considered in structuring an association site.

One technique that is being more widely adopted is use of a user agreement that establishes jurisdiction and venue. "Click-wrap" agreements calling for disputes to be resolved in a particular state applying the laws of that state have been upheld even in instances where a plaintiff objected because he did not scroll down his computer screen to read it. It is useful to post a User Agreement or Terms of Use at your site, and to include a provision on jurisdiction is useful. Many such agreements also require that disputes be referred to arbitration. Forum selection clauses can never insure that an association will not be sued—and certainly cannot insure that you will not be sued in a distant state—but may give you an opportunity to dismiss such a suit or to seek removal to a more convenient location.

XI. TAXES

No discussion of the Internet is complete without a mention of taxes. Taxation questions sometimes present thorny issues for associations in the United States. Adding to that the further intricacies of foreign tax laws, which may differ from U.S. laws governing nonprofit organizations, can be a nightmare. Consequently, this is merely a brief overview of some of the special tax issues associated with e-commerce.

The international nature of e-commerce has made developing a tax structure capable of balancing the complex needs of consumers, governments, and businesses an extraordinary challenge. The United States has responded by adopting the Internet Tax Freedom Act in 1998,[44] a law which imposes a moratorium on new taxes on e-commerce for a three year period, which expires October 21, 2001. Some legislators have called for an extension of the moratorium. Given the thousands of state and local sales taxes on goods and services, how to implement tax policy is difficult. Yet, facing the potential of significant loss in tax revenues as e-commerce grows, governors of various states have expressed concern and are developing a plan to address the situation. The issue is particularly crucial to states which rely solely or primarily on sales tax revenues.

The situation is complicated further by the Value Added Tax (VAT) structure common in the EU and elsewhere. The EU is developing a proposal to address this, which could multiply complexities for e-marketers, particularly in light of the existing

---

[44]26 USC § 513.

"country of destination" approach already reflected in the E-Commerce Directive where consumer sales are concerned.

Taxation of online sales is only one issue. Tax issues may be raised by certain B2B ventures, and the structure of those ventures can be a critically important element. Another tax issue for associations involves the generation of unrelated business income (UBIT). Advertising revenues may be subject to UBIT, for example, and revenues generated from Internet advertising will be no exception. The topic of UBIT alone, of course, is a subject of considerable complexity for associations. Special analyses by your financial and legal experts may be needed to assess the appropriate tax treatment of revenues generated from e-commerce activities.

Tax considerations should be part of your negotiating strategy in structuring linking, affiliation, and various e-commerce agreements. Many e-commerce agreements involve a variety of sometimes diverse payment schemes. Associations may receive a fee for their sponsorship or endorsement, granting the other party rights to post the association logo on a linked site and to use the name and logo in promoting an e-commerce opportunity. Agreements may also specify that the association must provide a variety of benefits to the business partner, such as free or discounted advertising in association publications, free or discounted booth space at conferences and trade shows, free or discounted meeting attendance, or opportunities to present seminars and other programs to members. The association may receive a flat fee for its sponsorship, a percent of net receipts on sales to members, a fee for hits on the linked site, and/or other payment options. The combination of fees may be subject to different tax treatment.

A "qualified sponsorship payment" (QSP) is a payment for corporate sponsorship and is tax-free if made by an organization engaged in a trade or business for which the organization will not receive a substantial benefit (other than the use of the association's name or logo).[45] If an association receives a substantial return benefit in exchange for payment, however, under proposed Internal Revenue Service regulations, the portion attributable to the substantial return benefit is not a QSP.[46] It may be useful to specify separately fees for various activities or arrangements to take advantage of QSP opportunities, remembering that new proposed regulations may affect the ultimate tax treatment for the payments involved.[47]

[45]26 U.S.C §513(i).
[46]IRS REG-209601-92. 1.513-4(c)(2)(ii)(A)(2)
[47]Rule proposed at 65 Fed. Reg.11012 (2000) (to be codified at 26 C.F.R § 1.513-4) (proposed Mar.1, 2000).

XII. CONCLUSION

This brief overview has merely scratched the surface of some of the most important legal issues associated with the Internet for nonprofit associations. As the Internet becomes more closely integrated into the daily lives of both businesses and consumers worldwide, resolving the policy and legal issues created by the Internet is becoming a higher priority for all associations, complicated in particular by the still-evolving jurisdictional conundrum. Associations have every stake in harnessing the vast potential of the Internet for the benefit of their members and organizations. Understanding the legal issues will help assure that your Internet ventures meet your objectives.

Appendix A

IP Do's and Don'ts

Understanding the difference between various types of IP is vital for associations, who rely on their information and brand identity in serving members. In the era of electronic communications, it is even more important to understand the differences between trademarks, copyrights, and trade secrets. Associations should utilize appropriate agreements, incorporate appropriate notices, and file for legal protection of important IP. The following do's and don'ts should make understanding these distinctions a bit easier.

TRADEMARK DO'S AND DON'TS

- How do I protect my trademarks?
    - ✔ do consider the benefits of federal trademark registration for important marks
    - ✔ do have your trademark attorney conduct a clearance search prior to adopting a proposed mark, and promptly register them
    - ✔ do explore possible domain names which match your proposed trademark prior to adopting a proposed mark
    - ✔ do execute trademark licenses when entering a B2B or affinity agreement, or administering certification or accreditation programs involving use of your logo
    - ✔ do provide written guidelines or license agreements to control member use of your marks (*e.g.*, limiting use on products, limits on signs, Web site guidelines etc.)
    - ✔ don't waste time and money by failing to have a trademark search conducted prior to the decision to adopt, use, and attempt to register an important new trademark

✔ don't prepare and file trademark applications or respond to objections raised by the U.S. Patent and Trademark Office without consulting your trademark counsel

✔ don't change the design, appearance, or wording of a registered trademark without consulting your trademark counsel

■ How do I use my trademarks?

✔ do use the ™ symbol for unregistered trademarks

✔ do use the ® symbol for registered trademarks

✔ do use the mark exactly as it appears in your registration

✔ do use your trademark consistently on labels, advertising, publications, packaging, and your Web site

✔ do use trademarks as adjectives (*i.e.*, BAND-AID ® brand bandages)

✔ do use capital letters, bold print, or quotation marks to distinguish trademarks, (*i.e.* (MINUTE MAID ® brand orange juice)

✔ don't use a trademark as a noun (*i.e.*, a bowl of "Cheerios")

✔ don't use a trademark as a possessive (*i.e.*, "Sunkist's Freshness")

✔ don't pluralize a trademark, (*i.e.*, "Three Snapples")

✔ don't use trademark as a verb, (*i.e.*, "Xerox These Papers")

✔ don't use the ® symbol on an unregistered trademark

✔ don't permit a business partner or others to use your trademark in a manner implying joint ownership

■ How do I enforce my rights?

✔ do look for trademark uses which are confusingly similar to your own

✔ do watch for unauthorized uses of your trademark, particularly in certification or accreditation situations

✔ do have your trademark counsel send inquiry letters or cease and desist letters to potential or known infringers

✔ do enter into license agreements when authorizing use of your trademarks or logos

✔ do contact your trademark counsel if you have any question about the use or protection of your trademarks or about branding, labeling, and advertising strategy

✔ don't change any element of your mark without advising your trademark counsel and understanding the implications

✔ don't advertise your goods or services without discussing use of your trademark with your trademark counsel

 ✔ don't respond to any cease and desist letters without consulting your trademark counsel

 ✔ don't contact possible infringers without consulting your trademark counsel

COPYRIGHT DO'S AND DON'TS

- How do I use and protect my copyrights?
   - ✔ do enter into copyright agreements with those developing potentially copyrightable works
   - ✔ do register important works with the United States Copyright Office within 90 days of publication (sale, offer to sell, lending, lease, other transfer of ownership)
   - ✔ do put the symbol ©, the word Copyright, or the abbreviation Copr. on the work
   - ✔ do put the year(s) of publication on the work
   - ✔ do put the author's name on the work
   - ✔ do include the statement "All rights reserved"
- How do I make sure I have authority to use others' copyrighted material?
   - ✔ do make sure you have appropriate software licenses for your software
   - ✔ do execute model agreements if using pictures
   - ✔ do execute work for hire agreements with your Web developer and others
   - ✔ do obtain releases/waivers of "moral rights"
   - ✔ do execute copyright assignments or licenses when entering a B2B or other agreement

TRADE SECRET DO'S AND DON'TS

- How do I protect my trade secrets?
   - ✔ do execute confidentiality agreements
   - ✔ do keep your trade secrets a secret
   - ✔ do stamp your trade secrets confidential
   - ✔ do limit access to trade secrets by employees and others
   - ✔ do limit copying of member lists and other confidential information
   - ✔ do include confidentiality provisions in B2B and other agreements where you are sharing confidential information with a third party
   - ✔ don't allow employees to take trade secrets home
   - ✔ don't allow employees to e-mail trade secrets

Appendix B

Copyright Work for Hire Checklist

A copyright "work for hire" or assignment agreement or clause should be used any-time you hire outside firms or individual consultants who will develop any type of written, graphic, or visual materials, including software. That means that a work for hire or copyright assignment provision is an essential provision in almost every type of Web agreement. The agreement or provision should establish association owner-ship of all intellectual property created, confidentiality of valuable member data, and other information disclosed. And if they are stand-alone agreements, they should include provisions establishing the parameters of the work to be done as well as timelines, payment, and other standard provisions.

- Describe Content or Work being created
  - ✔ specify that all subcontractors providing Content are also covered
- Establish association rights to content
  - ✔ provide that Works are works for hire (if they fall in the work for hire class)
  - ✔ in the alternative, obtain an assignment of copyright
  - ✔ in the alternative, obtain license for life of copyright
  - ✔ address right to use individual contributions to a collective work
- Reserve rights
  - ✔ to copy, reproduce, modify, display, perform, translate, create derivative works
  - ✔ in all media now known or later invented
  - ✔ throughout the universe
  - ✔ with no further payment or other obligation to contributor
- Require release of moral rights

- Require contributor to obtain model releases (if applicable)
- Address confidentiality of data or information provided to create the Work
- Include noncompete clause (as needed)
- Require contributor to obtain licenses/assignments/work for hire agreements with subcontractors on your behalf
- Obtain warranty of originality and noninfringement
- Include term and termination provision
- Include clause on "independent contractor" status
    - ✔ specify contractor responsibility for payment of workers' compensation, unemployment, and so forth, especially if the contractor is an individual
- Provide for all applicable Copyright Act remedies

Appendix C

Checklist for Web Hosting Agreements

Most associations—indeed, most businesses—use an outside firm to host their Web site. Most associations are familiar with Web hosting agreements and understand that visitors to their Web site actually visit them at space rented on the host's server. The host allocates space on its server for the site. There are a number of standard technical specifications and other considerations that should be addressed in Web hosting agreements. Sites doing business internationally may also need to consider filing hosting agreements with national Data Protection Authorities (DPAs) to establish their control over the privacy of personal information collected and processed by the Web site.

Web host agreements should generally include:

- Description of services
  - ✔ technical requirements and specifications
  - ✔ 24/7 operation
  - ✔ maintenance (scheduled to limit interference with operation)
  - ✔ downtime
  - ✔ response time
- Warranty of up-to-date server, traffic capacity
- Access rights of association employees
- Costs and fees
  - ✔ monthly/annual
  - ✔ special fees for additional maintenance
  - ✔ cost items
- Guarantees of service
  - ✔ software upgrades and patches

- ✔ response to denial of service attacks
- ✔ anti-virus protection
- ✔ data security
- ✔ data backup and backup schedule
- ■ Data, content ownership
    - ✔ establish copyright ownership of site content
    - ✔ licenses for use
    - ✔ service usage statistics/user data rights
    - ✔ incorporate privacy language if needed for foreign DPAs
    - ✔ confidentiality of data
- ■ Domain name allocation
- ■ Term and termination
    - ✔ extension of term (purchase order)
    - ✔ termination for cause (nonpayment, insolvency, etc.)

Appendix D

Web Development Request For Proposal (RFP) Checklist

As Web design becomes more sophisticated, many associations are working on taking their site to the next generation of technology and offerings. It is often useful to issue a Request for Proposal (RFP) to several Web developers in order to get competitive bids for the work. As with any consultant relationship, mutual trust and an agreement on principles and objectives is key to a mutually successful and rewarding agreement that advances your member service goals. The RFP should establish the goals and requirements for the association Web site.

In the RFP you should clarify that you will require complete ownership of digitized content at the site, and include important dates and milestones. For example, if you must have a new offering up and running prior to an important association event, like a major conference or trade show, this should be spelled out. It is important to check references and navigate other sites developed by the consultant to evaluate their capability, and the suitability for your audience of other Web site designs they have worked on. It is also critical for your in-house IT personnel to feel confident and comfortable with the Web developer you select.

Below is a checklist of some important considerations when selecting a Web developer.

- Outline Web site objectives
- Address confidentiality/proprietary information
- Include noncompete provision if necessary
- Establish fee schedule/budget parameters
- Address hosting requirements (if applicable)
- Address maintenance requirements (if applicable)
- Address software/hardware upgrades

- Establish requirements for content updates
- Specify association ownership of content
- Outline operating system requirements
  - ✔ hardware
  - ✔ software
  - ✔ compatibility issues
  - ✔ search capabilities
  - ✔ data management requirements
  - ✔ metatags
- Discuss design
  - ✔ text only, graphics, streaming audio, streaming video
  - ✔ public/member only areas
  - ✔ e-mail requirements (listservers, e-mail newsletters, etc.)
  - ✔ e-commerce requirements (if any)
  - ✔ Web accessibility (to persons with disabilities)
  - ✔ advertising
- Deadlines
- Check references
- Review other sites

Appendix E

Checklist for Web Development Agreements

Web development agreements can be relatively simple or highly complex, depending on the scope of services. Sometimes these agreements include hosting, maintenance, and content development requirements. Sometimes they include e-commerce development aspects. Consequently, development agreements must usually be carefully tailored to the specific needs of the site. Elements that should be addressed contractually may include:

- Description of services
    - ✔ hosting, maintenance
    - ✔ Web "look and feel"
    - ✔ consistency with other association materials (newsletters, etc.)
    - ✔ technical requirements (hardware and software, browser compatibility)
    - ✔ content (articles, graphics, streaming audio or video)
    - ✔ advertising capability
    - ✔ interactivity levels (e-mail updates, registrations, printer-friendly menus, "send a friend," etc.)
    - ✔ e-commerce capabilities
    - ✔ data management (rights to user data, integration with membership database)
    - ✔ storyboard/navigational blueprint development
    - ✔ site map
    - ✔ beta site/acceptance testing
- IP ownership
    - ✔ domain name, trademarks, copyrights, patents, trade secrets

✔ copyright work for hire/assignment provisions

✔ licenses for use of domain name, trademark, copyright, patents, trade secrets

✔ originality, noninfringement warranties/guarantees for content contributions by developer

✔ originality, noninfringement warranties/guarantees for content contributions by association

✔ rights to visitor, click stream data

✔ rights to digitized association content

- Key personnel
    ✔ include "services of the essence" clause as needed

- Confidentiality and nondisclosure
    ✔ carefully identify trade secret data—avoid overbroad description
    ✔ ensure association business plans, financial information, member lists, visitor data protected
    ✔ carefully consider implication of restrictions on "use"
    ✔ require return/destruction upon termination

- Exclusivity and noncompete provisions
- Duty to identify, update, software used to make site available
- Costs and fees
    ✔ performance milestones and payment schedule
    ✔ limits/approval for out-of-pocket expenditure
    ✔ "most favored customer" rates
    ✔ preapproval requirements for subcontracts
    ✔ right to withhold payments for failure to perform
    ✔ holdback until completion of tasks/projects

- Approval mechanisms and timing
    ✔ "time of the essence" (developer)
    ✔ "time of the essence" (association)
    ✔ absolute discretion of association to approve/disapprove content
    ✔ developer adherence to association content guidelines
    ✔ storyboards/navigational blueprints
    ✔ site map
    ✔ beta or shadow site testing requirements

- Site and data-security requirements
- Term and termination
    ✔ term may depend on developer role in ongoing content, updates

- ✔ provision for extension
- ✔ termination for cause (failure to perform, failure to pay, insolvency, other)
- ■ Miscellaneous
  - ✔ limitations of warranty
  - ✔ indemnification/hold harmless
  - ✔ jurisdiction/venue
  - ✔ independent contractor status
  - ✔ Alternative Dispute Resolution clause

Appendix F

B2B Antitrust Checklist

In considering whether to enter into or initiate a B2B venture involving your association, there are a number of key questions to ask. B2B arrangements could create potential anticompetitive conditions or situations if they are not carefully structured. Moreover, the evolution of an e-marketplace may create new issues, as new investors who receive shares in the company, new participants in the e-marketplace, new offerings, and new fee arrangements enter the picture. Ownership alone by a market participant may not create cause for concern. Control over the e-marketplace, access to transactional data, exclusivity requirements, minimum or maximum purchase requirements, and IP and information ownership, may cause concern, depending on the situation. The owner's position in offline sales and distribution markets is relevant as well.

Even if those types of issues do not raise antitrust concerns, they are relevant to the likely confidence that buyers and sellers will have in the marketplace, and, thus, to the potential future success of a B2B venture. Consequently, it is essential for associations to carefully consider the structure and operational features of a B2B marketplace before lending support to it.

Here are some of the questions to consider:

- Ownership
  - ✔ Who are the major equitable owners?
  - ✔ What is their role in offline sales, distribution channels?
  - ✔ What governance rights do equitable owners have in the B2B?
  - ✔ Are owners or potential owners actual or likely participants in the e-marketplace involved?
  - ✔ If so, are mechanisms in place to separate decision making by individual market participant in the market from decision making in the e-marketplace?

- ✔ Are owners providing products or services (*e.g.*, software, IP, hardware, Web hosting, consulting services, etc.) to the B2B e-marketplace or participants?
- ✔ Are key personnel employed by or affiliated with marketplace participants?

- Governance
  - ✔ Is the e-marketplace specifically designed to be buyer-oriented, seller-oriented, or neutral?
  - ✔ Is the governance structure dominated by buyers or sellers?
  - ✔ What provisions are in place to maintain the orientation of the marketplace (*e.g.*, neutral marketplace) in light of new investors/owners?
  - ✔ What specific transaction data are available to equitable owners and managers who might also be market participants?
  - ✔ If participation by market participants is permitted, what safeguards are in place to prevent the board of directors or other governing bodies from becoming unfairly unbalanced?

- Outsourced product and service providers
  - ✔ Are owners eligible to provide products and services to the e-marketplace or to e-marketplace participants?
  - ✔ Are "most favored customer" prices charged?
  - ✔ Does access to information about outsourced products and services (*e.g.*, shipping, logistics, etc.) create potential anticompetitive issues?

- Options for buying and selling
  - ✔ Are traders required to subscribe? Are different fees imposed on association members versus nonmembers?
  - ✔ Are purchases and sales available via a directory or list? Auction (open or closed)? Reverse auction? Closed bid?
  - ✔ Does the site offer credit checks?
  - ✔ Does the site set up trading accounts?
  - ✔ Does the site establish buyer/seller approval mechanisms before their employees may participate, or limit participation to designated employees?
  - ✔ Does the site assist in preclearing qualified bidders?

- Architecture
  - ✔ Is the site easily navigable?
  - ✔ Is specialized hardware or software required by a user?

- Fees (direct and indirect)
  - ✔ What fees are imposed (*e.g.*, transaction fees, participation or subscription fees, advertising fees, consulting fees, other)?

✔ Are discounts available for association members and for volume purchases?

✔ Is use of specific IP, software, or hardware required to participate?

✔ Does the e-marketplace offer consulting services to assist in back-end setup on an exclusive basis?

■ Fairness

✔ Are fees nondiscriminatory?

✔ What safeguards are in place to prevent collusion among buyers or sellers?

✔ Is exclusivity required?

✔ Are minimum/maximum purchases required?

✔ Do buyers and sellers have equal access to information?

✔ Do buyers and sellers have equal access to products and services?

■ Confidentiality

✔ Who has access to individually identifiable transaction data? Aggregate transaction data?

✔ Who has access to individually identifiable sales or purchase trend data? Aggregate purchase trend data?

✔ Who has access to registration data client lists?

✔ Is information available to owners for direct marketing of their products or services?

✔ Is information sold or rented to third parties for direct marketing?

✔ Is information collected on customer satisfaction/dissatisfaction? If so, is it available to traders?

■ Data security

✔ What mechanisms are in place to prevent denial of service attacks, hacking?

✔ Is access to individual transaction data by employees, agents of the B2B limited to those with a need to know?

✔ Is transaction data maintained as confidential business information?

■ Transparency

✔ Is information about ownership and governance readily available (including affiliations with entities providing outsourced products or services)?

✔ Are subscription and fee agreements available?

✔ Is information on buyers and sellers presented uniformly?

✔ Are complaints shared with the company involved? Others?

Appendix G

Web Site
User Agreement/Terms of Use

Most commercial sites post a User Agreement, Terms of Use, or Terms of Service to address a variety of legal issues associated with Web site use. These agreements are structured as license agreements, much as software "shrinkwrap" agreements are license agreements. Web site user agreements are less common on association Web sites than on commercial Web sites, but should be considered essential liability-limiting tools for all organizations operating Web sites. These sorts of agreements have been found to be enforceable in the United States. Depending on the content and activities of the site, consideration might be given to using "click to agree" mechanisms requiring the Web visitor to affirmatively acknowledge the existence of the terms of use before entering the site or participating in certain features.

Elements of a user agreement include provisions that:

- Establish that users are bound by the Terms of Service
- Identify the owner/operator of the site
- Include necessary copyright/trademark/patent ownership notices
- Address rights to ideas posted at the site
- Disclaim liability or responsibility for content of linked sites (member or nonmember) or public postings
- Disclaim intent that references to products or services constitute an endorsement
- Provide grant of license for noncommercial use
- Include or incorporate by reference chat room rules
- Include "as is" language—no warranties that site is always available, that use will be noninterrupted, or virus or error-free
- Disclaim warranties of merchantability, fitness for purpose

- Establish remedies for e-commerce (if applicable, *e.g.*, return/refund policies)
- Hold harmless provision
- Establish choice of law/venue
- Include Alternative Dispute Resolution clause (depending on offerings at the site)
- Provide contact information

Remember, however, that posting basic terms and conditions of use, even when structured as an agreement, does not mean that associations can ignore good practices in terms of reviewing claims and offerings. Due diligence remains one of the key liability-limiting tools available to any association.

Appendix H

Chat Room Rules

Chat rooms, bulletin and message boards, and "ask an expert" areas help build communities and can strengthen loyalty to your association. But chat rooms may create new and fuzzy legal liability risks, including liability for libel or defamation, interference with business advantage, employment discrimination or harassment, and IP infringement. New antitrust risks may also arise. Chat room rules should therefore be adopted to minimize liability. It is useful to adopt a "click to agree" feature for these rules, and to incorporate by reference your Terms of Use or User Agreement.

It is rare for associations to knowingly offer chat features for children. Associations that do, however, should take precautions and consider issues and requirements of the obligations governing commercial Web sites under the Children's Online Privacy Protection Act (COPPA), even if not legally required to do so.

Chat room rules can thus appear on a registration page (before a visitor clicks on a "submit" or "I agree" button) and can also be linked at the home page or chat areas of your site. Depending on the activities at the site, your chat room rules should address the following Do's and Don'ts, and include additional language set forth below:

- Do adhere to our antitrust guidelines when participating in any public forum at this site [link to your antitrust guidelines].
- Do use good judgment and good taste in your postings. All information you post is available for all to see, and we cannot restrict or limit its use by other parties.
- Do not post content that is harassing, threatening, obscene, or otherwise objectionable.
- Do not use this space to advertise or promote your own products or services.

[Note: this is especially important for sites that offer classified ads, because postings could detract from advertising revenue.]

- Do be sure that your postings do not violate the IP rights of others.
- Do remember that you are solely responsible for your postings.

In addition to these rules, all visitors must adhere to our Terms of Service/User Agreement [link], which contain additional rules governing use of this Site. [Association] does not monitor or control the content on any chat, message board, or bulletin board. Without in any way undertaking an obligation to review the content, however, [Association] may edit or delete any postings, or deny or restrict access to anyone using these areas in violation of our rules. We will also investigate misuse of our site and will cooperate in any such investigation by legal authorities or others.

Appendix I

Privacy Checklist

Privacy and security of data are emerging issues. Consumers—including business consumers—are concerned about potential identity theft, misuse of personal information, loss of confidentiality, and receipt of unsolicited information. In fact, spam is becoming a key concern of business users of the Internet. Associations, who traditionally deal primarily with their members, often zealously guard their member lists, but have been slow to focus on the issue of online privacy. With growing public and international focus on privacy, good business practice suggests that associations (particularly those dealing with consumers) should adopt privacy policies that generally address the following issues:

■ **WHO** is collecting personally identifiable information at the site?
   ✔ identify the organization operating the site
   ✔ provide e-mail and physical contact information
   ✔ establish whether other third parties (Web hosts, third party advertisers, business partners, etc.) may collect or access personal information at the site

■ **FROM WHOM** will information be collected?
   ✔ members only
   ✔ members of the public (including consumers)
   ✔ children (consider Children's Online Privacy Protection Act requirements)

■ **WHAT** personally identifiable and other information is collected through the Web site?
   ✔ describe, generally, the personal information collected and why
   ✔ describe passive information collection practices (use of cookies, Web beacons, etc.)

- ✔ take special precautions in dealing with young children (under age 13)
- ✔ remind visitors that chat room message board or bulletin board postings are available for others to see

■ **HOW** is the information used?
- ✔ used to fulfill orders (conference and trade show registration, product sales to members or others), etc.

■ **WITH WHOM** will the information be shared?
- ✔ disclose data-sharing arrangements with for-profit business partner and with charitable/educational organizations (including subsidiaries)

■ **WHAT CHOICES** are available to Web visitors regarding the collection, use and distribution of the information (*e.g.*, opt-out, opt-in)?
- ✔ describe any applicable opt-out or opt-in procedures, rights to access information, etc.

It is extremely important that you implement procedures to assure adherence to your privacy policy. Changes in how you handle data that differ from posted policies may be actionable.

Appendix J

Employee Electronic Communications Policy Checklist

It is important for all employers to develop policies on the use of electronic communications in the workplace. Electronic communications can be the source of claims about workplace harassment or discrimination. Employee abuse may also extend to using an employer's electronic system for illegal purposes. Rights to monitor should be specified to clarify that employees do not have a reasonable expectation of privacy in their office communications.

Policies should address:

- The primary business purposes of your business communications systems (telephone, voice mail, e-mail, Internet access, Web site, etc.)
- The employer's right to monitor electronic communications by employees
- The fact that attempts to use passwords, or to delete messages, may not fully eliminate the information from the association's system
- Procedures for reporting policy violations to management
- The employer's intent to investigate any reasonable allegation of misuse of its electronic communications system
- The fact that violations of the policy may result in disciplinary action, up to and including termination
- The employer's intent to cooperate with legal authorities as needed

In implementing this program, employers should:

- Train employees on their electronic communications policy
- Use filters to prevent employee access to inappropriate Web sites
- Enforce software license agreement provisions internally
- Investigate misuse (including complaints about employee e-mail, accessing improper sites, misuse of your system for potential illegal activity, etc.)
- Understand current monitoring procedures

- Limit monitoring to work-related, supervisory quality control activities, system integrity oversight, investigations of alleged infractions
- Limit disclosure to those who have a "need to know"